About the Author

As an accomplished Digital Marketing Specialist with 7 years of experience, I have navigated the dynamic landscape of marketing with precision and creativity. My diverse skill set encompasses photography, graphic design, copywriting, social media management, and SEO, allowing me to craft compelling narratives and engage diverse audiences effectively.

My passion lies in leveraging digital platforms to drive brand visibility and enhance corporate marketing and communications efforts. Through hands-on experience and a deep understanding of marketing principles, I empower businesses to thrive in today's competitive market.

In this journey, I present the 'Foundations of Marketing Handbook,' a comprehensive guide designed for students, professionals, and inquisitive minds seeking a solid understanding of marketing essentials. This concise yet detailed handbook provides a thorough overview of fundamental marketing principles, offering a gateway for those eager to attain foundational expertise.

Tailored to be accessible and informative, this resource covers core concepts, strategies, and insights essential for success in the dynamic field of marketing. Whether you're a student delving into the world of business or a professional expanding your skill set, this handbook serves as the perfect starting point, laying the groundwork for further exploration and practical application.

Uncover the building blocks of effective marketing and empower yourself with the knowledge needed to navigate this exciting realm with confidence.

TABLE OF CONTENTS

- **Chapter 1:** Unlocking the Essence: What is Marketing?
- **Chapter 2:** The Power of Purpose: Why Marketing Matters
- **Chapter 3:** Understanding Target Audiences
- **Chapter 4:** Navigating the Maze: Differentiating Marketing, Sales, and Advertising
- **Chapter 5:** Journey Through Time: Unraveling the History of Marketing
- **Chapter 6:** Classic vs. Contemporary: Traditional Marketing in the Modern Era
- **Chapter 7:** Digital Dawn: Embracing Modern Marketing in the Digital Age
- **Chapter 8:** Crafting Identity: The Power of Branding
- **Chapter 9:** Words That Sell: The Art of Copywriting
- **Chapter 10:** AI in Action: The Intersection of Marketing and Artificial Intelligence
- **Chapter 11:** Facts Unveiled: Insights into Marketing Realities
- **Chapter 12:** Quotable Wisdom: Best Quotes About Marketing
- **Chapter 13:** Legendary Figures: Icons of the Marketing World
- **Chapter 14:** Agency Spotlight: The Ogilvy Case Study
- **Chapter 15:** Strategic Prowess: Companies with Exceptional Marketing Strategies
- **Chapter 16:** How Budget Allocation Correlates with Marketing Success
- **Chapter 17:** Campaign Chronicles: Best Marketing Campaigns Case Studies
- **Chapter 18:** Resources for Continuous Learning and Professional Development
- **Chapter 19:** Data-driven Insights: Research Findings in the World of Marketing
- **Chapter 20:** Educational Eminence: World's Top Marketing Schools and their Success Stories

FOUNDATIONS OF MARKETING: YOUR HANDBOOK TO NAVIGATE THE MARKETING LANDSCAPE

Written By: NATASHA ABLE

Embark on your marketing journey with the **'Foundations of Marketing Handbook,'** a comprehensive guide designed for students, professionals, and inquisitive minds seeking a solid understanding of marketing essentials.

This concise yet detailed handbook provides a thorough overview of fundamental marketing principles, offering a gateway for those eager to attain a foundational expertise. Tailored to be accessible and informative, this resource covers core concepts, strategies, and insights essential for success in the dynamic field of marketing.

Whether you're a student delving into the world of business or a professional expanding your skill set, this handbook serves as the perfect starting point, laying the groundwork for further exploration and practical application.

Uncover the building blocks of effective marketing and empower yourself with the knowledge needed to navigate this exciting realm with confidence.

Chapter 1

UNLOCKING THE ESSENCE: WHAT IS MARKETING?

Defining Marketing and its Core Principles

At its core, marketing is the strategic and dynamic discipline that orchestrates the connection between businesses and their audiences. It is the art and science of understanding, creating, communicating, and delivering value to satisfy the needs of a target market. Let us dissect this multifaceted concept into its fundamental components.

• Strategic Connection: Marketing serves as the linchpin that aligns a company's offerings with the desires and needs of its target audience. It goes beyond mere transactions, aiming to build lasting relationships and loyalty.

• Understanding Customer Needs: At the foundation of marketing lies a profound comprehension of customer needs and desires. This involves continuous research, data analysis, and an empathetic understanding of consumer behavior to anticipate and fulfill their requirements.

• Value Creation: Marketing is the conduit through which businesses transform their products or services into valuable propositions. This value extends beyond the functional aspects, encompassing emotional and experiential dimensions that resonate with consumers.

• Communication and Messaging: Effective marketing is synonymous with compelling communication. It involves crafting messages that not only convey information but also resonate emotionally with the target audience. Storytelling, emotional appeal, and persuasive language are integral elements in this facet of marketing.

• Strategic Concepts: The Marketing Mix (4Ps): The marketing mix comprises four foundational elements — Product, Price, Place, and Promotion. It is a strategic framework that businesses employ to craft a cohesive and effective marketing strategy.

Each "P" represents a critical aspect, from defining the product offering to determining its price, deciding where it will be available, and promoting it to the target audience.

• Segmentation, Targeting, and Positioning (STP): To navigate the diverse landscape of the market, businesses engage in segmentation (dividing the market into distinct groups), targeting (choosing specific segments to serve), and positioning (creating a distinctive image in the minds of the target audience). These strategies enable businesses to tailor their offerings to specific consumer groups effectively.

In summary, marketing is a dynamic process that involves understanding the intricacies of consumer behavior, creating value that transcends the tangible, and communicating strategically to build lasting connections. It employs a mix of analytical insights, creativity, and strategic planning to ensure that businesses not only meet but exceed the expectations of their audiences. As we unfold the chapters ahead, we will delve deeper into each of these facets, providing a comprehensive exploration of the fascinating world of marketing.

Exploring the Evolution of Marketing Concepts

Marketing is a dynamic field that has undergone a fascinating evolution, shaped by societal changes, technological advancements, and shifting consumer behaviors. To understand the present and anticipate the future, we must embark on a historical journey through the evolution of marketing concepts.

Early Beginnings: The Transactional Era

The roots of marketing can be traced back to ancient civilizations where the focus was on simple transactions. The marketplace served as the central hub where goods were exchanged, laying the foundation for the transactional nature of early commerce. The emphasis was on the exchange of tangible goods without much consideration for customer needs beyond basic functionality.

The Production Era: Supply-Driven Marketing

With the Industrial Revolution, the focus shifted to mass production. The production era saw businesses producing goods on a large scale, with the primary goal of efficiency and cost reduction. Marketing efforts were limited, and the prevailing belief was that quality products would naturally find buyers.

The Sales Era: Persuasion and Promotion

As markets became more saturated, the sales era emerged. Businesses realized the need to actively promote and sell their products to a wider audience. This period marked the rise of advertising and promotional campaigns, emphasizing persuasion to drive sales. The customer became a target for selling rather than a participant in the market.

The Marketing Concept: A Customer-Centric Shift

The mid-20th century witnessed a significant paradigm shift with the advent of the marketing concept. Businesses began to prioritize customer needs and wants, shifting from a product-centric to a customer-centric approach. Market research gained prominence, and companies started tailoring their products based on consumer feedback and preferences.

The Relationship Era: Building Long-Term Connections

Entering the late 20th century and beyond, marketing evolved into the relationship era. The focus expanded beyond individual transactions to building long-term relationships with customers. Customer relationship management (CRM) systems and loyalty programs emerged, emphasizing the importance of retaining existing customers and fostering brand loyalty.

The Digital Age: Marketing in the Technological Revolution

The rise of the internet and digital technologies marked another pivotal moment in the evolution of marketing. The digital age brought about a seismic shift in how businesses connect with their audiences. Social media, content marketing, and data analytics became integral components, allowing for more personalized and targeted marketing strategies.

Integrated Marketing: Harmonizing Traditional and Digital Channels

In the contemporary landscape, marketing has embraced an integrated approach. Businesses leverage both traditional and digital channels to create a cohesive and comprehensive brand presence. Integrated marketing communications (IMC) ensure a unified message across various touchpoints, fostering a seamless customer experience.

As we navigate through the evolution of marketing concepts, it becomes evident that adaptability and responsiveness to changing landscapes are at the core of successful marketing strategies. Understanding this historical tapestry equips us with valuable insights as we delve into the complexities of modern marketing in the subsequent chapters.

Chapter 2

THE POWER OF PURPOSE: WHY MARKETING MATTERS

Unveiling the Significance of Marketing in Business and Society

In the grand tapestry of business and society, marketing stands as a powerful force that transcends the transactional exchange of goods and services. This chapter delves into the profound impact of marketing, unraveling why it matters on both business and societal levels.

The Strategic Engine of Business:

Marketing is the strategic engine that propels businesses forward, influencing their growth, success, and sustainability. At its core, marketing is about creating value and communicating that value effectively to the target audience. By identifying and satisfying customer needs, businesses not only survive but thrive in the competitive landscape.

Creating Brand Identities:

A central tenet of marketing lies in the creation and cultivation of brand identities. Brands are not merely logos or slogans; they are powerful symbols that carry meaning and associations. Effective marketing shapes these identities, fostering connections between businesses and consumers that extend beyond functional attributes to emotional resonance.

Fostering Innovation:

Marketing serves as a catalyst for innovation. By understanding customer preferences and market trends, businesses can innovate their products and services to meet evolving needs. Marketing research becomes the compass guiding organizations towards groundbreaking solutions and ensuring relevance in a dynamic environment.

Driving Economic Growth:

The ripple effect of marketing extends beyond individual businesses to contribute to the broader economy. As businesses flourish through effective marketing strategies, they generate employment, stimulate production, and contribute to overall economic growth. Marketing, therefore, becomes a key driver in fostering vibrant and sustainable economies.

Navigating Societal Trends:

Beyond its impact on individual businesses, marketing is deeply intertwined with societal trends and cultural shifts. It reflects and shapes societal values, influencing perceptions and contributing to the discourse on social issues. Businesses engaged in purpose-driven marketing can lead societal change by aligning with causes that resonate with their audience.

Consumer Empowerment:

Marketing empowers consumers by providing them with choices and information. Through transparent communication and targeted messaging, consumers are equipped to make informed decisions that align with their values. Marketing, when done ethically, ensures a balanced power dynamic between businesses and consumers.

Global Connectivity:

In the interconnected global landscape, marketing serves as a bridge that connects diverse cultures and communities. It facilitates cross-cultural communication, breaking down geographical barriers and fostering a sense of shared experiences. Brands with a global presence leverage marketing to build connections that transcend borders.

Social Responsibility:

As businesses become more conscious of their impact on the world, marketing plays a pivotal role in promoting social responsibility. Purpose-driven marketing campaigns address pressing societal issues, from environmental sustainability to social justice, positioning businesses as agents of positive change.

As we unravel the layers of the power of purpose in marketing, it becomes clear that marketing is not merely a business function; it is a transformative force with the potential to shape the trajectory of both commerce and society. Understanding this significance lays the groundwork for businesses to wield marketing as a tool for positive influence and lasting impact.

Understanding the Impact of Effective Marketing on Growth

Effective marketing serves as the catalyst for business growth, influencing not only financial metrics but also the overall trajectory and sustainability of an organization. In this section, we explore how strategic and impactful marketing contributes to robust growth in multifaceted ways.

Market Penetration and Expansion:

One of the primary ways effective marketing fuels growth is through market penetration and expansion. By identifying untapped segments, reaching new audiences, and enhancing brand visibility, businesses can penetrate existing markets and expand into new ones. This strategic expansion is often fueled by targeted campaigns, product innovation, and a deep understanding of consumer needs.

Brand Equity Enhancement:

A strong and well-managed brand is a powerful asset that directly impacts business growth. Effective marketing cultivates brand equity by shaping positive perceptions, fostering trust, and establishing emotional connections with consumers. Brands with high equity enjoy customer loyalty, premium pricing capabilities, and increased market share, all of which contribute to sustained growth.

Customer Acquisition and Retention:

Marketing plays a pivotal role in acquiring new customers and retaining existing ones. Strategic campaigns that resonate with target audiences attract new consumers, while ongoing engagement and relationship-building efforts ensure customer loyalty. The combination of customer acquisition and retention efforts creates a steady inflow of revenue and sets the stage for sustainable growth.

Innovation and Adaptability:

In the dynamic business landscape, innovation and adaptability are paramount for growth. Marketing research and feedback mechanisms provide insights into emerging trends and changing consumer preferences. By leveraging these insights, businesses can innovate their products, services, and marketing strategies to stay ahead of the curve, fostering a culture of continuous improvement and adaptability.

Competitive Advantage:

Effective marketing positions businesses to gain a competitive edge in their respective industries. Through differentiation strategies, businesses can highlight unique value propositions and set themselves apart from competitors. This competitive advantage not only attracts customers but also creates barriers to entry for new entrants, solidifying the business's position in the market.

Financial Performance Enhancement:

The impact of effective marketing is evident in enhanced financial performance. Increased brand visibility, customer loyalty, and market share directly contribute to revenue growth. Moreover, well-executed marketing strategies can optimize cost structures, improve profit margins, and generate a positive return on investment, amplifying the financial impact on business growth.

Crisis Resilience:

In times of crises or economic downturns, businesses with effective marketing strategies are better positioned to weather the storm. A strong brand and customer loyalty cultivated through strategic marketing efforts provide a buffer against adverse market conditions. Moreover, businesses can use marketing creatively to communicate resilience, empathy, and adaptability during challenging times, fostering trust and customer support.

Global Expansion Opportunities:

For businesses eyeing global growth, effective marketing is a key driver. Strategic international marketing campaigns, cultural adaptation, and a nuanced understanding of diverse markets open doors for global expansion. This global reach not only broadens the customer base but also diversifies revenue streams, reducing dependence on specific markets.

As we unravel the impact of effective marketing on growth, it becomes apparent that marketing is not merely a functional aspect of business but a dynamic force that propels organizations toward sustained and impactful expansion. The strategic interplay of marketing elements influences market dynamics, consumer perceptions, and overall business resilience, laying the foundation for robust and enduring growth.

Chapter 3

UNDERSTANDING TARGET AUDIENCES

Identifying, Segmenting, and Selecting Target Audiences

In the realm of marketing, success hinges on the ability to forge meaningful connections with target audiences. This chapter explores the intricate art of understanding, identifying, segmenting, and selecting target audiences – a cornerstone in creating campaigns that resonate on a personal level.

Understanding Target Audiences:

Before a connection can be made, a deep understanding of the target audience is imperative. This involves delving beyond demographic data to unravel the psychographic nuances that define consumer behaviors, preferences, and aspirations. By immersing in the mindset of the audience, marketers can craft messages that resonate authentically and cultivate lasting connections.

Identifying Target Audiences:

The process of identifying target audiences begins with market research and data analysis. It involves studying consumer demographics, psychographics, and behavioral patterns to pinpoint the individuals or groups most likely to be receptive to the brand's offerings. Through this meticulous identification, marketers lay the groundwork for creating tailored and impactful campaigns.

Segmentation Strategies:

Once identified, target audiences are often diverse, necessitating segmentation strategies for more effective communication. Segmentation involves grouping consumers based on shared characteristics, needs, or behaviors. From demographic segmentation to psychographic and behavioral segmentation, marketers employ various strategies to tailor their messages to specific segments, ensuring relevance and resonance.

Psychographic Profiling:

Psychographic profiling delves into the psychological and emotional aspects of the target audience. This involves understanding their values, beliefs, interests, and lifestyles. By constructing detailed psychographic profiles, marketers gain insights into the emotional triggers that drive consumer decisions. This deeper understanding enables the creation of campaigns that align seamlessly with the audience's aspirations and motivations.

Behavioral Analysis:

Understanding consumer behavior is fundamental to effective targeting. Behavioral analysis involves studying how consumers interact with products, their purchasing patterns, and responses to marketing stimuli. By analyzing these behaviors, marketers can predict future actions, tailor messages to specific behavioral triggers, and optimize campaigns for maximum impact.

Geographic Considerations:

In a globalized world, geographic considerations remain pivotal in target audience strategies. Cultural nuances, regional preferences, and localized trends significantly influence consumer behaviors. Through geographic segmentation, businesses can tailor their offerings and marketing messages to resonate with the unique characteristics of specific regions, fostering a sense of local relevance.

Selecting Target Audiences:

The final step in the process is the strategic selection of target audiences. This involves prioritizing segments based on factors such as market potential, alignment with brand values, and growth opportunities. By selecting target audiences strategically, marketers optimize resource allocation, ensuring that campaigns are directed toward segments with the greatest potential for engagement and conversion.

As we navigate the realms of understanding, identifying, segmenting, and selecting target audiences, it becomes clear that effective targeting is the bedrock of successful marketing. This chapter serves as a guide for marketers to embark on a journey of profound connection, ensuring that every campaign resonates with the hearts of the intended audience.

Strategies for Effective Audience Engagement

In the dynamic landscape of marketing, audience engagement stands as the heartbeat of successful campaigns. This section explores comprehensive strategies designed to captivate, resonate, and foster meaningful connections with target audiences.

1. Content Relevance and Personalization:

Tailoring content to the specific needs and preferences of the audience is paramount for engagement. Personalization goes beyond addressing the audience by name; it involves delivering content that speaks directly to their challenges, aspirations, and interests. By understanding the unique nuances of each segment, marketers can create content that resonates on a personal level.

2. Interactive Campaigns and Experiences:

Engagement thrives on interactivity. Campaigns that invite participation, whether through polls, quizzes, contests, or interactive content, encourage audience involvement. Interactive experiences not only capture attention but also create a sense of involvement, transforming passive observers into active participants in the brand narrative.

3. Social Media Activation:

Social media platforms provide a dynamic stage for audience engagement. Marketers can leverage the interactive features of platforms like Instagram, Twitter, and Facebook to initiate conversations, share behind-the-scenes glimpses, and respond directly to audience queries. Building a community through social media fosters a sense of belonging and connection.

4. Storytelling with Emotional Resonance:

Stories have the power to evoke emotions, and emotional resonance is a cornerstone of engagement. Craft narratives that not only convey information but also tap into the emotional spectrum of joy, empathy, or inspiration. Stories that align with the audience's values and experiences create a lasting impact, forging a deeper connection.

5. Multi-Channel Campaigns:

Engagement is not confined to a single channel. Multi-channel campaigns ensure that the brand reaches the audience where they are most active. From email marketing to social media, blogs, and events, a cohesive and synchronized approach across multiple channels enhances brand visibility and provides diverse touchpoints for audience interaction.

6. User-Generated Content Integration:

Harnessing the power of user-generated content involves encouraging customers to create and share content related to the brand. This not only showcases genuine interactions but also amplifies the brand's reach through authentic recommendations. Incorporating user-generated content into marketing campaigns creates a sense of community and shared ownership.

7. Surveys and Feedback Loops:

Creating avenues for direct feedback is an integral part of audience engagement. Surveys, polls, and feedback loops provide a platform for the audience to voice their opinions. Actively listening to this feedback not only demonstrates a commitment to customer satisfaction but also guides future campaigns based on audience preferences.

8. Influencer Collaborations:

Collaborating with influencers who resonate with the target audience can be a powerful engagement strategy. Influencers bring authenticity and credibility, bridging the gap between brands and consumers. Carefully chosen influencers align with the brand's values, creating an organic connection that enhances audience trust.

9. Gamification:

Incorporating elements of gamification into campaigns adds an element of fun and excitement. Gamified experiences, such as quizzes, challenges, or reward-based activities, not only capture attention but also create a sense of enjoyment and accomplishment, fostering positive associations with the brand.

10. Real-Time Engagement:

Timeliness is crucial for engagement. Responding promptly to comments, messages, and trends in real-time demonstrates an active and responsive brand. Real-time engagement not only keeps the audience involved but also positions the brand as attentive to their needs and current industry conversations.

As we delve into the strategies for effective audience engagement, it becomes evident that successful engagement is a dynamic and multifaceted endeavor. By combining personalization, interactivity, and a deep understanding of audience preferences, marketers can craft campaigns that not only capture attention but also nurture lasting connections with their target audience.

Chapter 4

NAVIGATING THE MAZE: DIFFERENTIATING MARKETING, SALES, AND ADVERTISING

Clarifying Distinctions Between Marketing, Sales, and Advertising

In the intricate landscape of business communication, the terms marketing, sales, and advertising are often used interchangeably, leading to confusion. This chapter seeks to unravel the distinct roles and functions of marketing, sales, and advertising, offering clarity on their unique contributions to the overall business strategy.

1. Marketing: The Strategic Architect

At its core, marketing is the strategic architect of the business landscape. It encompasses a holistic approach that goes beyond selling products or services. Marketing is about understanding the market, identifying target audiences, creating compelling messages, and fostering long-term connections. It lays the groundwork for sales by creating awareness, generating leads, and cultivating brand loyalty.

2. Sales: The Transactional Maestro

Sales, on the other hand, is the transactional maestro. It involves the direct interaction with customers to convert leads into purchases. The sales process is focused on individual transactions, negotiations, and closing deals. While marketing builds the foundation, sales teams execute the strategies to meet revenue goals, emphasizing personal relationships and direct engagement with potential buyers.

3. Advertising: The Amplifier of Messages

Advertising is the amplifier that brings the brand message to a wider audience. It is a subset of marketing that involves creating and disseminating promotional content through various channels. Advertising aims to create awareness, shape perceptions, and drive interest in the brand. It works in tandem with marketing strategies but has a distinct focus on crafting compelling messages for mass communication.

4. Marketing's Strategic Lifecycle:

Marketing operates across the entire lifecycle of a product or service. From the initial stages of market research and product development to creating brand awareness, generating leads, and fostering customer loyalty, marketing strategies span the entire business journey. It is a continuous and strategic effort that adapts to market changes and evolving consumer needs.

5. Sales' Tactical Execution:

Sales, in contrast, is more tactical and transactional. It comes into play at specific stages of the customer journey, focusing on converting leads into customers and ensuring the successful completion of individual transactions. Sales teams employ personalized approaches, negotiation skills, and relationship-building to guide prospects through the purchasing process.

6. Advertising's Creative Expression:

Advertising is the creative expression of the brand message. It utilizes various mediums such as print, digital, television, or social media to communicate with a broad audience. Advertising campaigns are designed to capture attention, convey brand values, and evoke emotional responses. While aligned with marketing objectives, advertising specifically concentrates on crafting visually impactful and compelling messages for mass consumption.

7. Collaboration for Synergy:

For optimal results, marketing, sales, and advertising need to work collaboratively. Marketing lays the groundwork and creates the overall strategy, advertising amplifies the messages to a broader audience, and sales teams execute the personalized interactions to convert prospects into customers. The synergy between these functions ensures a cohesive and effective business approach.

8. Metrics and Measurement:

Marketing, sales, and advertising have distinct metrics for measurement. Marketing success is often gauged through metrics like brand awareness, lead generation, and customer engagement. Sales teams focus on conversion rates, revenue generated, and customer acquisition costs. Advertising success is measured by reach, impressions, and the impact on brand recall. Each function contributes specific data points that collectively provide a comprehensive view of overall business performance.

By understanding the nuances of marketing, sales, and advertising, businesses can optimize their strategies for maximum impact. This chapter serves as a compass, providing clarity on the distinct roles these functions play within the broader business framework, ensuring a harmonious orchestration of efforts for sustained success.

Understanding their Complementary Roles in Business Success

While marketing, sales, and advertising operate as distinct functions, their true power lies in the seamless synergy they create when working together. This section explores the complementary roles of marketing, sales, and advertising, highlighting how their collaborative efforts orchestrate a symphony of success for businesses.

1. Marketing as the Architectural Blueprint:

Marketing sets the stage for success by creating the foundational blueprint for business strategies. It involves in-depth market research, identification of target audiences, and crafting comprehensive plans that extend throughout the product lifecycle. Marketing lays the groundwork for sales and advertising, providing a strategic direction that aligns with overall business objectives.

2. Advertising as the Amplifier of Messages:

Advertising steps onto the stage as the amplifier of messages crafted by marketing. It takes the strategic narratives and brand values developed by marketing and brings them to life through creative and visually compelling campaigns. Advertising serves as the megaphone that broadcasts the brand message to a wider audience, creating awareness and generating interest that fuels the sales pipeline.

3. Sales as the Tactical Execution:

Sales teams pick up the baton at a tactical level, executing personalized interactions to convert leads into customers. Informed by the strategic groundwork laid by marketing and amplified by advertising, sales professionals engage directly with prospects. They utilize negotiation skills, build relationships, and guide individuals through the purchasing journey, transforming marketing strategies into tangible business transactions.

4. Seamless Customer Journey:

The collaboration between marketing, sales, and advertising ensures a seamless customer journey. Marketing introduces the brand, advertising amplifies the messages, and sales teams engage personally with customers. This holistic approach creates a cohesive and positive experience for consumers, from the initial brand awareness stage to the final transaction, fostering brand loyalty and customer satisfaction.

5. Data Sharing for Continuous Improvement:

Effective collaboration relies on data sharing and continuous improvement. Marketing collects data on customer behaviors, preferences, and market trends. Sales teams contribute valuable insights from direct customer interactions. Advertising effectiveness is measured through various metrics. This shared data ecosystem allows each function to refine and adapt its strategies, ensuring a dynamic response to changing market dynamics.

6. Collective Metrics for Comprehensive Evaluation:

The collective success of marketing, sales, and advertising is measured through a spectrum of metrics that provide a comprehensive evaluation of business performance. While marketing looks at brand awareness, lead generation, and engagement metrics, sales focuses on conversion rates, revenue generation, and customer acquisition costs. Advertising metrics include reach, impressions, and impact on brand recall. Together, these metrics offer a holistic view that guides strategic decisions for future campaigns.

7. Customer Feedback Loop:

A collaborative approach encourages the establishment of a robust customer feedback loop. Insights gathered from customer interactions, whether through marketing surveys, sales feedback, or responses to advertising campaigns, become invaluable for refining strategies. This loop fosters a culture of customer-centricity, ensuring that business efforts align with evolving customer needs and preferences.

By understanding and embracing their complementary roles, marketing, sales, and advertising become integral components of a cohesive and effective business strategy. The synergy between these functions not only amplifies the impact of each individually but also propels the business toward sustained success by creating a unified and positive brand experience for customers.

Chapter 5

JOURNEY THROUGH TIME: UNRAVELING THE HISTORY OF MARKETING

In this chapter, we embark on a fascinating journey through the annals of history to explore the origins and evolution of marketing practices. From ancient civilizations to the modern era, we'll uncover the key milestones that have shaped the dynamic landscape of marketing, providing valuable insights into the foundations of this essential business discipline.

Tracing the Roots of Marketing:

Marketing, in its essence, is as old as commerce itself. The roots of marketing can be traced back to the earliest human civilizations, where traders and merchants sought to promote their goods and services in bustling marketplaces. In ancient Mesopotamia, Egypt, and Greece, artisans and merchants utilized rudimentary forms of advertising, such as signage and word-of-mouth, to attract customers and drive sales.

The Birth of Modern Marketing:

The concept of modern marketing began to take shape during the Renaissance period, a time of intellectual and cultural rebirth in Europe. With the rise of mercantilism and the expansion of trade routes, merchants and artisans found themselves competing in increasingly crowded marketplaces. Innovations such as the printing press enabled the mass production of advertising materials, allowing businesses to reach wider audiences with their marketing messages.

Key Milestones in the History of Marketing

The Industrial Revolution:

The 18th and 19th centuries saw the advent of the Industrial Revolution, a period of rapid technological advancement and economic growth. With the mechanization of production processes, goods could be manufactured on a scale never before imagined, leading to the rise of mass production and mass marketing. Marketing strategies evolved to meet the demands of this new industrial age, with the emergence of branding, advertising agencies, and market research.

The Golden Age of Advertising:

The 20th century witnessed the rise of advertising as a dominant force in shaping consumer behavior. From the iconic campaigns of the "Mad Men" era to the proliferation of television and radio advertising, brands sought to capture the attention of consumers through compelling storytelling and visual imagery. Advertising became increasingly sophisticated, as marketers employed psychology and behavioral science to influence consumer perceptions and preferences.

The Digital Revolution

The advent of the internet and digital technologies heralded a new era of marketing innovation and disruption. With the rise of e-commerce, social media, and digital advertising, marketers gained unprecedented access to consumer data and insights. Digital marketing strategies such as search engine optimization (SEO), content marketing, and email marketing revolutionized the way businesses engage with their audiences, offering new opportunities for targeted advertising and personalized messaging.

Further Explorations: Essential Reading on the Evolution of Marketing

"The History of Marketing Science" by Terrence W. Anderson and Dana L. Alden

- This comprehensive book traces the development of marketing as a discipline from its origins to the present day, exploring key theories, concepts, and practices.

"The Evolution of Marketing" by Walter J. Ferrier

- Offering a historical perspective on marketing, this book examines how marketing has evolved over time in response to changing social, economic, and technological factors.

"Advertising and Society: An Introduction" by Carol J. Pardun

- This textbook explores the historical and cultural impact of advertising, examining its role in shaping consumer behavior, popular culture, and societal norms.

"The Marketing Century: How Marketing Drives Business and Shapes Society" edited by Jerome McCarthy and William D. Perreault Jr.

- This anthology provides a comprehensive overview of the evolution of marketing over the past century, featuring contributions from leading scholars and practitioners in the field.

"Brand Warfare: 10 Rules for Building the Killer Brand" by David D'Alessandro

- While primarily focused on branding, this book offers valuable insights into the historical context of marketing, exploring how brands have evolved and adapted to changing consumer preferences and market dynamics.

"The Ultimate History of Advertising: From Ancient Times to the Present Day" by Martyn Ford and David Brown

- This visually stunning book traces the history of advertising from its earliest origins to the modern era, showcasing iconic campaigns, advertisements, and branding strategies throughout history.

"Mad Men and Bad Men: What Happened When British Politics Met Advertising" by Sam Delaney

- Focusing on the intersection of advertising and politics, this book explores how advertising techniques have been used to shape public opinion, influence elections, and advance political agendas throughout history.

"The Consuming Instinct: What Juicy Burgers, Ferraris, Pornography, and Gift Giving Reveal About Human Nature" by Gad Saad

- While not strictly a history book, this insightful exploration of consumer behavior provides valuable context for understanding the historical roots of marketing and advertising.

As we trace the history of marketing from its ancient origins to the digital age, we gain a deeper understanding of the foundations of this essential business discipline.

By studying the key milestones and pivotal moments that have shaped the evolution of marketing practices, we can gain valuable insights into the strategies and techniques that continue to drive success in the modern marketplace.

Chapter 6

CLASSIC vs. CONTEMPORARY: TRADITIONAL MARKETING IN THE MODERN ERA

Defining Traditional Marketing Approaches

In the ever-evolving landscape of marketing, traditional approaches have paved the way for modern strategies, creating a dynamic interplay between classic and contemporary methodologies. This section delves into the foundations of traditional marketing, unraveling its defining approaches and shedding light on its enduring impact in the modern era.

1. Print Media: The Timeless Chronicle

Traditional marketing traces its roots to the tangible pages of print media. Newspapers, magazines, brochures, and direct mail were stalwarts in reaching target audiences. These channels allowed businesses to convey messages through carefully crafted copy, visuals, and advertisements. The enduring nature of print media lies in its tangibility, offering a physical connection with the audience.

2. Broadcast Advertising: Capturing Audiences through Airwaves

Before the digital age, broadcast media reigned supreme. Television and radio advertisements became iconic components of traditional marketing. Television commercials brought visuals and storytelling to living rooms, creating memorable brand experiences. Radio, with its auditory allure, captured audiences through jingles and engaging narratives. These classic mediums shaped cultural landscapes and left an indelible mark on marketing history.

3. Outdoor Advertising: Billboards and Beyond

The streets became a canvas for traditional marketers through outdoor advertising. Billboards, posters, and transit advertisements strategically positioned in high-traffic areas aimed to capture the attention of passersby. The static yet impactful nature of outdoor advertising made it a cornerstone of traditional marketing, providing a constant visual presence in the physical environment.

4. Telemarketing: Direct Conversations in a Connected World

In the era before digital communication, telemarketing emerged as a direct and personal approach to connect with potential customers. Businesses engaged in one-on-one conversations via phone calls, pitching products or services directly to individuals. While its effectiveness led to widespread use, evolving consumer preferences and regulations have reshaped the landscape of telemarketing in the contemporary era.

5. Events and Sponsorships: Building Brand Presence Offline

Traditional marketing found expression through live events and sponsorships. From trade shows and conferences to sports and cultural events, businesses sought to build brand presence through direct interactions with audiences. Sponsorships of events and activities aligned with the brand's values, creating associations that extended beyond the confines of traditional advertisements.

6. Direct Mail: Personalized Outreach in Physical Form

Direct mail became a hallmark of traditional marketing, allowing businesses to send personalized messages directly to the mailboxes of target audiences. Direct mailers, catalogs, and promotional materials provided a tangible touchpoint for consumers. While the digital age has transformed communication channels, the concept of personalized, physical outreach remains relevant in certain industries.

7. Print Advertising: Crafting Visual Narratives

Print advertising extended beyond newspapers and magazines to include posters, flyers, and other visual materials. Businesses leveraged the power of graphic design and compelling visuals to convey messages in a concise and impactful manner. The art of crafting visual narratives in print advertising left an indelible mark on the collective memory of consumers.

8. Catalog Marketing: Showcasing Product Offerings

Catalogs were a classic tool in the traditional marketing arsenal, particularly in retail. Businesses meticulously curated catalogs showcasing their product offerings, allowing consumers to peruse a comprehensive collection at their leisure. While digital catalogs have gained prominence, the tangible experience of flipping through pages persists as a nostalgic aspect of traditional marketing.

As we define the approaches of traditional marketing, it becomes evident that these classic strategies have woven themselves into the fabric of marketing history. While the contemporary era embraces digital innovations, the enduring influence of traditional approaches continues to shape the multifaceted landscape of marketing in the modern era.

Adapting Traditional Strategies to the Digital Age

As the digital age transforms the marketing landscape, the evolution of traditional strategies becomes imperative for relevance and effectiveness. This section explores the nuanced process of adapting classic marketing approaches to the dynamic realm of the digital era, leveraging the strengths of both worlds for a harmonious and impactful presence.

1. Digital Print Media: Transforming Pages into Pixels

The essence of print media has seamlessly transitioned into the digital realm. Digital newspapers, e-magazines, and online brochures have emerged as dynamic platforms, providing interactive and immersive experiences. Marketers can now harness the power of multimedia, hyperlinks, and responsive design to create engaging digital publications that transcend the limitations of traditional print.

2. Online Video Advertising: The Evolution of Broadcast

The rise of online video platforms has redefined the landscape of broadcast advertising. Marketers can now create compelling video content for platforms like YouTube, Vimeo, and social media channels. The digital space allows for precise targeting, real-time analytics, and the flexibility to experiment with various video formats, revolutionizing how brands engage with audiences through moving visuals.

3. Digital Outdoor Advertising: From Billboards to Screens

Outdoor advertising has found a new home in the digital era. Electronic billboards, interactive screens, and augmented reality experiences in urban spaces have transformed traditional static messages into dynamic, real-time interactions. Digital outdoor advertising embraces the advantages of technology, allowing marketers to adapt messages swiftly and tailor content based on location, time, and audience demographics.

4. Social Media Marketing: The Contemporary Telemarketing

Social media platforms serve as the contemporary counterpart to traditional telemarketing. Businesses engage with audiences through direct messaging, comments, and interactive content. Social media offers a two-way communication channel, enabling brands to build relationships, address customer inquiries, and cultivate a community in a manner reminiscent of the direct conversations in the era of telemarketing.

5. Virtual Events and Sponsorships: The Digital Gathering

In the digital age, live events and sponsorships have transcended physical boundaries. Virtual conferences, webinars, and online sponsorships enable businesses to connect with global audiences. The immersive experience of digital events allows for real-time engagement, networking, and brand exposure, mirroring the essence of traditional events in an increasingly interconnected world.

6. Email Marketing: The Digital Direct Mail

Email marketing is the digital incarnation of direct mail strategies. Businesses can personalize messages, tailor content based on customer behavior, and segment audiences for targeted campaigns. The strategic use of email marketing ensures that businesses maintain direct communication with their audience, just as direct mail once delivered personalized messages to physical mailboxes.

7. Interactive Digital Catalogs: A Virtual Showcase

Digital catalogs offer an interactive and immersive experience that extends the legacy of print catalogs into the digital realm. Marketers can leverage multimedia elements, clickable links, and responsive design to create engaging digital catalogs accessible across various devices. The evolution from physical pages to virtual showcases enhances the user experience and expands the reach of product offerings.

8. Online Advertising: Crafting Digital Visual Narratives

The art of crafting visual narratives remains central in online advertising. Digital platforms provide expansive canvases for graphic design, storytelling, and interactive elements. From display ads to social media visuals, businesses can convey their brand messages creatively, ensuring a seamless transition from the visual storytelling heritage of traditional print advertising to the dynamic landscape of the digital era.

9. Websites as Digital Storefronts: The Evolution of Brochures

Websites have evolved into digital storefronts, resembling the informative and visually engaging nature of traditional brochures. Just as brochures provided comprehensive information about products or services, websites serve as dynamic platforms for businesses to showcase offerings, share company stories, and interact with audiences. Responsive design, multimedia content, and user-friendly interfaces transform websites into interactive hubs, ensuring a seamless transition from the static nature of traditional brochures to the dynamic possibilities of the digital age.

10. SEO (Search Engine Optimization): Navigating the Digital Landscape

SEO functions as the contemporary compass in the digital landscape, akin to the strategic placement considerations of traditional outdoor advertising. In the digital realm, businesses strategically optimize their online presence to enhance visibility and rankings on search engine results pages. SEO involves tailoring content, utilizing keywords, and enhancing website structure to align with search algorithms. The goal is to ensure that businesses are prominently featured when audiences explore relevant topics, mirroring the strategic placement considerations of traditional outdoor advertising to capture attention in the digital realm.

11. Content Marketing: The Modern Narrative Crafting

Content marketing seamlessly integrates traditional storytelling principles with contemporary digital platforms. Much like the art of crafting narratives in print advertising, content marketing focuses on creating valuable, relevant, and consistent content to attract and engage target audiences. Blog posts, articles, infographics, and videos serve as digital counterparts to traditional content mediums. By delivering informative and compelling content, businesses cultivate trust, authority, and audience connection, echoing the timeless essence of narrative crafting in the digital age.

12. Digital Influencer Marketing: The Modern Word-of-Mouth

Influencer marketing in the digital realm mirrors the effectiveness of word-of-mouth recommendations in traditional marketing. Digital influencers, often prominent figures on social media platforms, collaborate with brands to endorse products or services to their followers. This form of marketing leverages the influencers' credibility and reach to create authentic connections with audiences. It draws parallels with traditional word-of-mouth strategies, where personal recommendations played a crucial role, but adapts to the digital age by harnessing the influence of online personalities to authentically promote products and services.

13. Mobile Marketing: The Pocket-Sized Revolution

Mobile marketing is a pivotal aspect that transcends the limitations of traditional marketing approaches. In the digital age, mobile devices serve as ubiquitous companions, presenting opportunities for targeted marketing strategies. From mobile-optimized websites and apps to location-based targeting and push notifications, mobile marketing encapsulates the tailored approach of traditional direct mail but in a pocket-sized, dynamic format. This facet ensures that businesses engage with audiences on a personal level through devices that have become integral to daily life.

By adapting traditional strategies to the digital age, businesses not only preserve the essence of classic marketing approaches but also unlock new dimensions of engagement, personalization, and data-driven insights. The integration of traditional wisdom with contemporary tools positions marketers to navigate the complexities of the digital era while retaining the time-tested principles that have shaped the world of marketing.

Chapter 7

DIGITAL DAWN: EMBRACING MODERN MARKETING IN THE DIGITAL AGE

The Emergence and Dominance of Digital Marketing

The evolution of marketing has witnessed a transformative shift with the emergence and subsequent dominance of digital marketing. This subsection explores the pivotal moments in the rise of digital marketing, tracing its roots, and unraveling the factors that have propelled it to the forefront of contemporary marketing strategies.

1. Birth of the Internet: Pioneering a New Era

The inception of the internet marked a revolutionary moment in the marketing landscape. As the world became digitally interconnected, businesses gained a global platform to reach audiences. The transition from traditional mediums to digital channels opened unprecedented possibilities for instantaneous communication, information dissemination, and interactive engagement.

2. Rise of Search Engines: Navigating the Digital Landscape

The advent of search engines, led by pioneers like Google, reshaped how information was accessed and discovered. Search Engine Optimization (SEO) emerged as a critical aspect of digital marketing, allowing businesses to optimize their online presence for visibility. The rise of search engines transformed the way consumers sought information, laying the foundation for a more targeted and user-centric approach.

3. Social Media Revolution: Connecting Beyond Boundaries

The social media revolution propelled digital marketing into a new era of connectivity. Platforms like Facebook, Twitter, Instagram, and LinkedIn transformed how businesses interacted with audiences. Social media marketing became a dynamic avenue for brand promotion, customer engagement, and the amplification of messages through shares and likes. The real-time, conversational nature of social media ushered in an era where brands and consumers engaged in direct, immediate communication.

4. Mobile Revolution: Marketing on the Move

The widespread adoption of smartphones ushered in the mobile revolution, fundamentally altering how consumers accessed information. Mobile marketing emerged as a cornerstone, emphasizing the importance of mobile-optimized websites, apps, and location-based services. The pocket-sized nature of mobile devices introduced the concept of marketing on the move, reaching audiences wherever they were, at any given moment.

5. Evolution of E-Commerce: Digital Storefronts

The evolution of e-commerce platforms reshaped the retail landscape. Digital marketing became intricately linked with online shopping experiences, with platforms like Amazon, eBay and Alibaba taking the lead. Businesses could leverage digital channels to not only promote products but also facilitate seamless transactions. The integration of e-commerce into digital marketing strategies revolutionized the way consumers discovered, evaluated, and purchased products and services.

6. Data-Driven Marketing: Insights for Precision

Digital marketing brought forth a wealth of data-driven insights. Analytical tools and platforms allowed businesses to gather, analyze, and interpret data related to consumer behaviors, preferences, and interactions. The era of data-driven marketing ushered in a new level of precision, enabling businesses to tailor campaigns, measure performance, and optimize strategies based on real-time information.

7. Automation and AI: Streamlining Marketing Processes

The incorporation of automation and artificial intelligence (AI) revolutionized marketing workflows. From email marketing automation to chatbots and personalized recommendations, automation technologies streamlined repetitive tasks, enhanced customer experiences, and allowed marketers to focus on strategic initiatives. The infusion of AI brought predictive analytics, machine learning, and personalized targeting to the forefront, shaping a more sophisticated and efficient approach to digital marketing.

As we delve into the emergence and dominance of digital marketing, it becomes evident that this evolution has not merely been a technological shift but a fundamental restructuring of how businesses connect with their audiences. The digital age has introduced a dynamic, interconnected ecosystem, reshaping the very fabric of marketing strategies and opening avenues for innovation and engagement that were once beyond imagination.

Navigating Various Digital Marketing Channels

In the expansive landscape of digital marketing, businesses navigate through a diverse array of channels to engage audiences, build brand presence, and drive conversions. This subsection provides an in-depth exploration of key digital marketing channels, shedding light on their unique characteristics, strategic applications, and the dynamic interplay that collectively forms a comprehensive digital marketing strategy.

1. Search Engine Marketing (SEM): The Gateway to Visibility

Search Engine Marketing (SEM) stands as a cornerstone of digital visibility. It encompasses paid advertising on search engines, prominently displayed alongside organic search results. Businesses leverage platforms like Google Ads to bid on keywords, ensuring their offerings are prominently featured when users actively search for relevant products or services. SEM provides immediate visibility and is crucial for capturing audience intent during the search process.

2. Social Media Marketing: The Conversational Hub

Social Media Marketing harnesses the power of popular platforms like Facebook, Instagram, Twitter, and LinkedIn to connect with audiences on a personal level. Businesses create tailored content, engage in conversations, and leverage targeted advertising to reach specific demographics. The conversational nature of social media fosters community-building, brand loyalty, and amplification of messages through shares and interactions.

3. Content Marketing: Value-Driven Narratives

Content Marketing revolves around creating and distributing valuable, relevant content to attract and engage target audiences. Blog posts, articles, infographics, videos, and other formats serve as digital assets that not only inform but also build brand authority. Content marketing aims to provide value, answer user queries, and establish long-term relationships by consistently delivering meaningful narratives across various digital platforms.

4. Email Marketing: Direct Communication Channel

Email Marketing remains a powerful channel for direct communication with audiences. Businesses utilize newsletters, promotional emails, and personalized campaigns to nurture leads, retain customers, and convey important messages. The targeted nature of email marketing allows for tailored content delivery, ensuring that messages resonate with specific segments of the audience, ultimately driving engagement and conversions.

5. Influencer Marketing: Leveraging Online Credibility

Influencer Marketing taps into the credibility and reach of online personalities to endorse products or services. Businesses collaborate with influencers who align with their brand values to authentically promote offerings. Influencer marketing leverages the trust established between influencers and their followers, facilitating genuine connections that can significantly impact brand awareness, credibility, and consumer decision-making.

6. Video Marketing: Dynamic Visual Engagement

Video Marketing leverages the power of visuals to convey messages in a dynamic and engaging manner. Platforms like YouTube, TikTok, and Instagram provide spaces for businesses to share tutorials, product demonstrations, brand stories, and creative content. Video marketing captures attention effectively, communicates messages vividly, and caters to the growing preference for visual content consumption in the digital landscape.

7. Mobile Marketing: Tailored for On-the-Go Audiences

Mobile Marketing recognizes the prevalence of smartphones in daily life. It involves optimizing websites for mobile devices, creating mobile apps, and leveraging strategies like SMS marketing. Mobile marketing ensures that businesses reach on-the-go audiences with tailored content, location-based promotions, and seamless experiences designed for the unique attributes of mobile devices.

8. Display Advertising: Visual Impressions Across the Web

Display Advertising involves placing visual ads on websites, apps, and social media platforms to capture audience attention. These visual impressions include banner ads, interstitial ads, and rich media ads. Display advertising allows businesses to create visually compelling campaigns, target specific demographics, and increase brand visibility across the vast expanse of the digital landscape.

9. Affiliate Marketing: Collaborative Performance

Affiliate Marketing fosters collaboration between businesses and affiliates who promote products or services in exchange for a commission. It operates on a performance-based model, ensuring that affiliates are incentivized to drive sales and conversions. Affiliate marketing harnesses the influence of various partners, expanding reach and tapping into diverse audience segments through collaborative efforts.

10. Webinars and Virtual Events: Digital Engagement Platforms

Webinars and virtual events have become integral components of digital marketing, offering immersive experiences for audiences. Businesses host online events to showcase expertise, launch products, and engage with attendees in real-time. The interactive nature of webinars and virtual events fosters engagement, allows for audience interaction, and creates a sense of community in the digital sphere.

11. Chatbots and AI-Powered Assistance: Automated Interaction

Chatbots and AI-powered assistance streamline customer interactions by providing instant responses to inquiries and facilitating transactions. Businesses integrate chatbots into websites, messaging apps, and social media platforms to enhance customer support, answer frequently asked questions, and guide users through the customer journey. The automated nature of chatbots ensures efficiency in handling routine queries, leaving room for human agents to address more complex issues.

As businesses navigate these various digital marketing channels, the strategic integration of these approaches forms a cohesive and dynamic marketing strategy. Each channel offers unique advantages and aligns with specific objectives, allowing businesses to tailor their digital presence according to the nature of their products, services, and target audiences.

Chapter 8

CRAFTING IDENTITY: THE POWER OF BRANDING

In this chapter, we delve into the transformative power of branding. From defining identity to shaping perceptions, we explore how branding influences consumer choices and fosters lasting connections.

Crafting Identity, Establishing Presence, and Fostering Connection

1. Defining Your Brand Identity: The Foundation of Recognition

Building a brand starts with a clear definition of its identity. We delve into the essential components, from establishing a mission and values to defining a unique proposition. This foundational step forms the bedrock for consistent and authentic brand communication that resonates with your target audience.

2. Target Audience Analysis: Tailoring Your Brand for Connection

Understanding your audience is pivotal. We explore methods for conducting thorough audience research, creating detailed buyer personas, and aligning your brand with the specific needs and preferences of your audience. Tailoring your brand to resonate authentically enhances its connection with consumers.

3. Strategic Brand Positioning: Carving Your Niche

Effective brand positioning sets your brand apart in the market. We delve into how to identify your brand's unique position, differentiating it from competitors. By strategically carving out a niche, you create a foundation for your brand to be perceived as distinctive, relevant, and valuable in the eyes of your audience.

4. Visual Branding Elements: Creating a Lasting Impression

Visual elements serve as the face of your brand. We discuss the strategic selection of logos, color schemes, and design elements that encapsulate your brand identity.

Crafting visually appealing and cohesive elements ensures a memorable and consistent brand image that resonates with your audience.

5. Crafting Brand Messaging: Communicating Your Story

The narrative of your brand is a potent tool. We explore the art of crafting compelling brand messages that align with your identity and resonate with your audience. From taglines to mission statements, effective messaging communicates your brand's story in a way that captures attention and fosters connection.

6. Consistency Across Channels: Reinforcing Brand Cohesion

Consistency is paramount in brand building. We discuss the importance of maintaining a cohesive brand image across various channels, from online platforms to offline materials. Reinforcing consistency builds brand recognition and strengthens the connection between your audience and your brand.

7. Building Brand Trust: The Pillar of Long-term Success

Trust is the bedrock of brand loyalty. We explore strategies for building trust, including transparent communication, quality consistency, and ethical practices. Establishing trust fosters customer loyalty and advocacy, contributing to the long-term success of your brand.

8. Evolving Your Brand: Adapting to Changing Landscapes.

A successful brand is agile and adaptable. We discuss the importance of evolving your brand to meet changing market trends, consumer behaviors, and industry landscapes. By staying responsive and relevant, your brand maintains its relevance and resonance over time.

By dissecting each facet of building a brand, from defining identity to fostering trust and adapting to change, this subchapter provides a comprehensive guide for crafting a brand that not only stands out but also resonates authentically with your audience, laying the foundation for long-term success.

The Role of Branding in Consumer Perception: Shaping Impressions, Influencing Choices, and Fostering Loyalty

Branding is a powerful force that goes beyond logos and visuals; it plays a central role in shaping how consumers perceive a company. In this subchapter, we explore the intricate dynamics of how branding influences consumer perception, delving into the psychology behind it, the factors that contribute to a positive brand image, and the strategies to navigate potential challenges.

1. The Psychology of Brand Perception: Unraveling the Consumer Mind

Consumer perception is a complex interplay of emotions, experiences, and brand interactions. We delve into the psychology behind how consumers form impressions, examining the role of cognitive processes, emotions, and the subconscious mind in shaping brand perception. Understanding these psychological nuances provides a foundation for intentional and strategic brand management.

2. Creating a Positive Brand Image: Consistency, Quality, and Values

A positive brand image is built on a foundation of consistency, quality, and shared values. We discuss how maintaining a consistent brand identity across touchpoints, delivering high-quality products or services, and aligning with values that resonate with your target audience contribute to fostering a favorable perception. Building a positive image is not only about visual appeal but also about delivering on promises and creating meaningful connections.

3. Emotional Branding: Forging Connections Beyond Functionality

Emotions play a significant role in brand perception. We explore the concept of emotional branding, where brands go beyond functional attributes to create emotional connections with consumers. By tapping into emotions such as joy, nostalgia, or trust, brands can foster a deeper and more enduring relationship with their audience, ultimately influencing how they are perceived.

4. Brand Trust: The Cornerstone of Positive Perception

Trust is a key element in how consumers perceive a brand. We discuss the factors that contribute to building and maintaining trust, including transparency, reliability, and ethical practices. Establishing trust not only enhances brand perception but also cultivates loyalty, as consumers are more likely to choose a brand they perceive as trustworthy.

5. Challenges in Brand Perception: Navigating Reputational Risks

While positive brand perception is a goal, challenges may arise. We explore common issues that can impact brand perception, from negative reviews to public relations crises. Understanding how to navigate and mitigate reputational risks is crucial for safeguarding the positive perception you've worked to build. Proactive strategies for crisis management and reputation repair are integral aspects of brand resilience.

By unraveling the psychology, strategies, and challenges associated with the role of branding in consumer perception, this subchapter provides a comprehensive guide for understanding and influencing how your brand is perceived in the eyes of your audience. From building trust to navigating challenges, it equips you with the knowledge needed to strategically manage and enhance brand perception for sustained success.

Chapter 9

WORDS THAT SELL: THE ART OF COPYWRITING

Crafting Compelling Copy that Converts

Copywriting is the art of using words to persuade, engage, and ultimately drive action. In this chapter, we explore the fundamental principles of effective copywriting, dissecting the techniques that transform words into powerful tools for conversion.

Crafting Compelling Copy through Scarcity, Social Proof, Authority, and Urgency

Effective copywriting is an intricate dance with the psychology of persuasion, and mastering it involves weaving four fundamental principles into the fabric of your narrative. In this subchapter, we dissect how scarcity, social proof, authority, and urgency serve as psychological triggers, creating a dynamic interplay that captivates audiences and compels them to take the desired actions.

1. Scarcity: Creating Desire through Exclusivity

Scarcity leverages the innate human fear of missing out (FOMO) to create desire. By emphasizing limited availability, whether in terms of product quantity, time-limited offers, or exclusive access, copywriters can instill a sense of urgency that propels audiences to act swiftly, driven by the fear of losing out on a valuable opportunity.

2. Social Proof: Harnessing the Power of Validation

Social proof capitalizes on the psychological principle that individuals look to others for validation and guidance. By incorporating testimonials, user reviews, and endorsements into copy, a sense of community and validation is established. This builds trust, reduces skepticism, and encourages readers to align their decisions with the positive experiences of others.

3. Authority: Influencing through Expertise

Authority involves positioning the brand or message as an expert or authoritative figure in the field. This can be achieved through showcasing credentials, certifications, expert endorsements, or demonstrating in-depth knowledge. By establishing credibility and expertise, copywriters can instill confidence in the audience, making them more receptive to the persuasive message.

4. Urgency: Tapping into the Fear of Missing Out (FOMO)

Urgency, often coupled with scarcity, prompts immediate action. By introducing time-sensitive elements, limited-time offers, or exclusive deals, copywriters create a psychological push that encourages readers to act promptly. Urgency taps into the fear of missing out, motivating individuals to make decisions swiftly to secure a perceived benefit.

5. Integrating Principles Seamlessly: Crafting a Persuasive Narrative

The art lies in not just understanding these principles individually but in seamlessly integrating them into the copy to form a persuasive narrative. An effective copy might employ scarcity to create desire, substantiate claims with social proof, establish authority to build trust, and instill urgency for immediate action. The delicate balance and strategic placement of these elements within the narrative are key to captivating audiences and compelling them towards the desired actions.

By delving into the psychology of persuasion and mastering the strategic application of scarcity, social proof, authority, and urgency, copywriters can craft narratives that resonate deeply with audiences, foster engagement, and drive meaningful conversions. This subchapter provides a comprehensive guide to leveraging these psychological principles effectively within the context of copywriting, offering actionable insights for creating compelling and persuasive content.

Crafting Compelling Copy through Audience Understanding, Persona Creation, and Strategic Language Tailoring

1. The Art of Market Research: Gaining Insights Before Words

Effective copy begins with a profound understanding of your audience. We delve into the art of market research, discussing methodologies such as surveys, data analysis, and customer feedback. By gaining comprehensive insights into demographics, behaviors, and preferences, you lay the groundwork for creating impactful and resonant copy.

2. Persona Creation: Breathing Life into Statistical Data

Audience personas are more than demographic labels; they're the living embodiments of statistical data. We explore the process of creating detailed and nuanced audience personas. From age and gender to interests and challenges, these personas personify your ideal reader, allowing you to address specific needs and motivations with a personalized touch.

3. Identifying Pain Points: Navigating Challenges for Solutions

Every audience grapples with challenges, and effective copy addresses these pain points head-on. We discuss techniques for identifying these challenges through customer feedback, market analysis, and social listening. Understanding the struggles and aspirations of your audience allows for the strategic incorporation of solutions and benefits within the copy.

4. Emotional Resonance: Speaking Directly to Aspirations

Effective copy goes beyond features and benefits; it taps into the emotional core of the audience. We explore the art of aligning your copy with the aspirations and desires of your intended readership. By connecting with the audience on a personal and emotional level, you create narratives that resonate deeply, fostering a sense of understanding, empathy, and relevance.

5. Language Tailoring: Precision in Communication

Language is a powerful tool, and its impact varies across demographics. We discuss strategies for tailoring language to specific age groups, cultural backgrounds, and communication preferences. Precision in communication enhances relatability, ensuring that your copy resonates authentically with the intended audience. From tone to terminology, we dissect the elements that contribute to precise and effective communication.

6. The Power of Storytelling: Creating Emotional Connections

Storytelling is a cornerstone of persuasive copywriting. We unravel the narrative techniques that engage emotions, build connections, and guide readers on a journey. Whether through anecdotes, testimonials, or brand narratives, storytelling transforms copy into a compelling narrative that resonates with audiences.

7. Clarity and Conciseness: The Art of Simplicity

In the digital age, attention spans are limited. We explore the importance of clarity and conciseness in copywriting, emphasizing the need to convey messages with precision. Clear, concise copy ensures that readers grasp the value proposition swiftly, reducing friction in the decision-making process.

8. Creating Irresistible Headlines and Hooks

Headlines and hooks serve as the entry point to captivating copy. We analyze the anatomy of irresistible headlines, exploring techniques such as curiosity, urgency, and benefit-driven statements. Crafting compelling hooks ensures that readers are enticed to delve further into the copy, setting the stage for conversion.

9. The Call to Action (CTA): Guiding the Next Step

Every effective piece of copy culminates in a compelling Call to Action (CTA). We break down the elements of a persuasive CTA, exploring language choices, positioning, and the psychological cues that prompt readers to take the desired actions. A well-crafted CTA serves as the culmination of the copywriting journey, driving conversions and engagement.

10. A/B Testing and Iteration: Refining Copy for Impact

The art of copywriting is an iterative process. We explore the importance of A/B testing, analyzing data, and refining copy based on performance metrics. Copywriters must be adaptable, continually optimizing language, structure, and messaging to align with audience responses and enhance overall effectiveness.

11. SEO and Copywriting: Balancing Visibility and Persuasion

In the digital landscape, copywriting must seamlessly integrate with Search Engine Optimization (SEO) strategies. We examine how to balance the need for visibility with the art of persuasion. Strategies include keyword optimization, user-friendly content structures, and maintaining a balance between search engine algorithms and human-centric readability.

12. Legal and Ethical Considerations: The Responsibility of Words

Copywriting comes with legal and ethical responsibilities. We discuss considerations such as truth in advertising, avoiding deceptive practices, and respecting intellectual property. Understanding the ethical dimensions of copywriting ensures that persuasive messaging aligns with integrity and transparency.

By delving into the art of copywriting and its nuanced techniques, marketers and advertisers will gain a comprehensive understanding of how words can be strategically crafted to not only captivate audiences but also guide them towards meaningful actions, making copywriting a powerful tool in the marketer's arsenal.

Unlocking the Principles of Persuasion, Engagement, and Conversion

1. Psychology of Persuasion: Unveiling the Influential Triggers

Effective copywriting is an intricate dance with the psychology of persuasion. We explore the principles that drive human behavior, from the scarcity mindset to the fear of missing out (FOMO). By understanding these influential triggers, you gain the insights needed to infuse your copy with persuasive elements that captivate and guide readers toward desired actions.

2. Emotional Resonance: Tapping into Deep Connections

Beyond rational arguments, effective copy taps into emotions. We dissect how emotions drive decision-making and explore techniques for creating an emotional resonance within your audience. From joy to fear, and from hope to urgency, we delve into the emotional spectrum that allows your copy to connect deeply and meaningfully with readers.

3. Cognitive Biases: Leveraging Mental Shortcuts

Human minds are prone to certain cognitive biases that influence decision-making. We unravel these biases, from confirmation bias to anchoring effect, and discuss how to leverage them strategically in your copy. By understanding how people naturally think and make decisions, you can align your messaging to match these cognitive patterns for enhanced persuasion.

4. The Power of Storytelling: Shaping Narratives for Impact

Storytelling is a timeless tool in effective copywriting. We explore the narrative techniques that create memorable stories, from relatable anecdotes to compelling brand stories. By mastering the art of storytelling, you can transform your copy into a journey that captivates, engages, and leaves a lasting imprint on the minds of your audience.

5. Behavior Change: Guiding Readers Toward Action

Effective copy doesn't just inform; it guides and influences behavior. We delve into behavioral psychology to understand how copy can lead readers through a journey of change. From crafting compelling calls to action to implementing behavior triggers, we dissect the strategies that empower your copy to be a catalyst for meaningful actions.

6. Neuromarketing Insights: Aligning Copy with Brain Responses

Neuromarketing provides insights into how the brain responds to marketing stimuli. We explore principles such as sensory appeal, visual hierarchy, and cognitive fluency. By aligning your copy with these neuromarketing insights, you can optimize its impact on the brain, ensuring that your message is not only seen but also processed and remembered.

7. User Experience: Enhancing Copy for Seamless Interaction

Copy is not just about words; it's an integral part of the user experience. We discuss how the psychology of user experience influences the effectiveness of your copy. From readability and information architecture to the strategic placement of content, we explore how user-centric principles enhance the overall impact and engagement of your copy.

By mastering the psychology of effective copywriting, you not only become a wordsmith but a strategist who understands the intricate dance between language and human behavior. This chapter provides a comprehensive guide, offering actionable insights and real-world examples to empower you in crafting copy that not only communicates but persuades, engages, and ultimately drives meaningful actions.

Masterful Moments: Decoding the Power of Copywriting in 10 Iconic Campaigns

1. Nike's "Just Do It":

Example: "Empowering and concise, 'Just Do It' inspires action, creating a brand identity rooted in motivation and determination."

2. Apple's "Think Different":

Example: "By urging consumers to 'Think Different,' Apple established a revolutionary brand image, associating innovation with individuality."

3. Coca-Cola's "Share a Coke":

Example: "Personalization at its best, 'Share a Coke' transformed a global brand into a personal experience, fostering a sense of connection and joy."

4. Volvo's "The Epic Split" (Jean-Claude Van Damme):

Example: "Demonstrating precision and innovation, Volvo's 'Epic Split' showcased their trucks' stability with jaw-dropping visuals, leaving an indelible mark on viewers."

5. FedEx's "When it Absolutely, Positively Has to Be There Overnight":

Example: "A slogan that promises reliability and urgency, FedEx's tagline instantly communicates their commitment to timely and secure deliveries.

6. M&M's "Melts in Your Mouth, Not in Your Hands":

Example: "Simple yet effective, M&M's memorable slogan emphasizes the product's quality and reinforces the mess-free pleasure of indulging in their chocolates."

7. Audi's "Vorsprung durch Technik" (Advancement through Technology):

Example: "Audi's tagline, in German, signifies innovation and superiority, positioning the brand as a leader in automotive technology."

8. McDonald's "I'm Lovin' It":

Example: "With its catchy jingle and positive sentiment, McDonald's 'I'm Lovin' It' captures the joyous essence of their brand, making it memorable worldwide."

9. Old Spice's "The Man Your Man Could Smell Like":

Example: "Old Spice's humorous and memorable campaign redefined the brand, targeting both men and women with a fresh, entertaining approach to personal care."

10. Amazon's "A to Z" Smile Logo:

Example: "Amazon's logo cleverly incorporates an arrow from 'A' to 'Z,' symbolizing their extensive product range and commitment to customer satisfaction, from start to finish."

In the realm of copywriting, these examples showcase the transformative impact of words. From Nike's motivational 'Just Do It' to Coca-Cola's personalized 'Share a Coke,' each brand demonstrates the art of crafting compelling narratives.

In the world of words, as in life, the right combination can spark movements and leave an enduring imprint.

Chapter 10

AI IN ACTION: THE INTERSECTION OF MARKETING AND ARTIFICIAL INTELLIGENCE

How AI is Revolutionizing Marketing Strategies

The marriage of marketing and Artificial Intelligence (AI) marks a transformative era, where data-driven insights, predictive analytics, and automation converge to reshape traditional marketing strategies. This subsection explores the profound impact of AI on marketing, unraveling the ways in which businesses harness intelligent technologies to enhance efficiency, precision, and the overall effectiveness of their marketing endeavors.

1. Data-Driven Decision Making: Precision Through Insights

AI empowers marketers with the ability to process vast amounts of data at incredible speeds. Machine learning algorithms analyze consumer behaviors, preferences, and interactions, providing invaluable insights. This data-driven approach enables marketers to make informed decisions, tailor campaigns to specific audience segments, and optimize strategies based on real-time feedback. The precision derived from AI-generated insights ensures that marketing efforts resonate more effectively with target audiences.

2. Predictive Analytics: Anticipating Consumer Trends

AI's predictive analytics capabilities elevate marketing strategies by forecasting future trends and consumer behaviors. By analyzing historical data patterns, AI algorithms can anticipate upcoming trends, preferences, and potential market shifts. Marketers leverage these predictions to proactively align campaigns, product launches, and content creation with anticipated consumer demands, thereby staying ahead of the curve in a rapidly evolving market landscape.

3. Personalization at Scale: Tailored Customer Experiences

AI unlocks the potential for hyper-personalization at scale, allowing businesses to tailor marketing messages and content based on individual preferences and behaviors.

Machine learning algorithms analyze customer data to understand unique preferences, predict future actions, and dynamically adjust content in real-time. Personalized experiences foster stronger connections with consumers, enhance engagement, and increase the likelihood of conversions by delivering content that resonates on a personal level.

4. Chatbots and Conversational AI: 24/7 Customer Interaction

AI-driven chatbots and conversational interfaces revolutionize customer interactions by providing instant, round-the-clock assistance. These intelligent systems simulate natural language conversations, addressing customer queries, guiding purchasing decisions, and facilitating transactions. Chatbots not only enhance customer satisfaction through prompt responses but also streamline operational efficiency by handling routine inquiries, allowing human agents to focus on more complex tasks.

5. Automated Content Creation: Efficiency in Campaigns

AI-powered tools enable automated content creation, streamlining the process of generating compelling visuals, written content, and marketing collateral. Natural Language Processing (NLP) algorithms can craft engaging copy, while AI-driven design tools generate visually appealing graphics. Automation in content creation accelerates campaign timelines, maintains consistency, and frees up creative teams to focus on strategic aspects, fostering efficiency and creativity in tandem.

6. Programmatic Advertising: Precision in Ad Campaigns

AI-driven programmatic advertising optimizes the placement of ads in real-time, ensuring that messages reach the right audience at the right moment. Automated algorithms analyze user data, behaviors, and demographics to deliver highly targeted and relevant advertisements across various digital channels. Programmatic advertising enhances ad efficiency, minimizes wasted ad spend, and maximizes the impact of campaigns through data-driven precision.

7. Dynamic Pricing Strategies: Adaptive Market Positioning

AI facilitates dynamic pricing strategies that adapt to market fluctuations, demand changes, and competitor pricing in real-time. Machine learning algorithms analyze diverse data sources, enabling businesses to set optimal prices based on current market conditions and consumer behaviors. Dynamic pricing ensures competitive positioning, maximizes revenue, and allows businesses to swiftly respond to evolving market dynamics.

8. Customer Journey Optimization: Seamless Experiences

AI optimizes the customer journey by analyzing user behaviors and interactions across multiple touchpoints. Machine learning models predict the most effective paths for conversions, enabling marketers to enhance user experiences, reduce friction points, and strategically position content at critical stages of the customer journey. By understanding the customer's path, businesses can optimize marketing efforts to guide users seamlessly toward conversion.

The revolution of marketing strategies through AI represents a paradigm shift in how businesses engage with audiences. By embracing the capabilities of Artificial Intelligence, marketers not only enhance efficiency and precision but also unlock innovative possibilities that elevate the overall impact of their strategies in an increasingly complex and data-driven digital landscape.

Examples of Essential AI Tools for Modern Marketing

To harness the transformative power of Artificial Intelligence in marketing, businesses often rely on a diverse array of cutting-edge tools. These tools streamline processes, enhance analytical capabilities, and unlock new dimensions of efficiency. Here's a curated list of commonly used AI tools that have become integral to modern marketing strategies:

1. Google AI Platform: Unleashing Machine Learning Capabilities

Google AI Platform provides a robust and scalable environment for businesses to build, deploy, and manage machine learning models. Marketers leverage this platform to implement predictive analytics, personalized recommendations, and other AI-driven applications seamlessly.

2. IBM Watson Marketing: Cognitive Insights for Marketing Strategies

IBM Watson Marketing integrates AI and cognitive computing to offer advanced analytics, predictive insights, and personalized customer experiences. Marketers use Watson Marketing to analyze large datasets, derive actionable insights, and enhance campaign strategies with cognitive capabilities.

3. Salesforce Einstein: AI-Powered Marketing Intelligence

Salesforce Einstein infuses AI into the Salesforce platform, offering marketers predictive analytics, automated lead scoring, and intelligent customer insights. This tool empowers marketers to make data-driven decisions, automate repetitive tasks, and deliver personalized experiences across the customer journey.

4. HubSpot's Marketing Hub: Automation and AI for Inbound Marketing

HubSpot's Marketing Hub integrates AI features, including lead scoring, predictive analytics, and automation, to enhance inbound marketing efforts. Marketers utilize HubSpot's AI capabilities to automate workflows, personalize content, and optimize interactions with leads and customers.

5. Adobe Sensei: AI for Creative and Marketing Solutions

Adobe Sensei serves as the AI and machine learning framework within Adobe's creative and marketing products. Marketers leverage Sensei to analyze data, automate creative tasks, and personalize content, enhancing the overall efficiency and effectiveness of Adobe's suite of marketing solutions.

6. Chatfuel: Chatbot Development for Conversational Marketing

Chatfuel is a user-friendly platform for building chatbots on messaging platforms like Facebook Messenger. Marketers utilize Chatfuel to create conversational AI experiences, automate customer interactions, and provide instant support, contributing to enhanced customer engagement.

7. Acquisio: AI-Powered Advertising Management

Acquisio is an AI-powered platform designed for managing and optimizing digital advertising campaigns. Marketers use Acquisio's machine learning algorithms to automate bid management, optimize ad performance, and enhance the overall efficiency of paid advertising efforts.

8. Albert: Autonomous AI for Marketing

Albert is an autonomous AI platform that leverages machine learning to optimize digital marketing campaigns across channels. Marketers employ Albert to automate tasks such as audience targeting, campaign optimization, and creative testing, allowing for continuous improvement and adaptation.

9. Optimizely: AI-Driven Experimentation and Personalization

Optimizely incorporates AI to facilitate experimentation, A/B testing, and personalization across digital experiences. Marketers use Optimizely to optimize website content, test variations, and deliver personalized experiences that resonate with diverse audience segments.

10. Peltarion: AI Platform for Deep Learning Applications

Peltarion is an AI platform focused on deep learning applications. Marketers leverage Peltarion to implement advanced deep learning models for tasks such as image recognition, natural language processing, and other complex AI-driven functionalities.

These AI tools represent a glimpse into the diverse ecosystem of technologies that empower marketers to navigate the complexities of the modern digital landscape. By integrating these tools into their strategies, businesses can unlock the full potential of AI and stay at the forefront of innovation in the dynamic field of marketing.

Chapter 11

FACTS UNVEILED: INSIGHTS INTO MARKETING REALITIES

Unearthing Surprising and Lesser-Known Facts about Marketing

In the dynamic world of marketing, uncovering hidden truths and lesser-known facts can provide marketers with a fresh perspective and a deeper understanding of the industry. Here, we unravel surprising insights that challenge conventional wisdom and unveil the intricacies of marketing realities:

1. The Power of Color Psychology:

• Fact: The choice of color in branding can significantly impact consumer perception and behavior.
• Insight: Colors evoke emotions and influence decision-making. Understanding the psychology behind colors empowers marketers to strategically shape brand identity and elicit specific responses from their target audience.

2. The Impact of Visual Consistency on Recognition:

• Fact: Consistent visual branding across channels can increase brand recognition by up to 80%.
• Insight: Visual consistency is a potent tool in creating a memorable brand presence. Marketers who maintain cohesive design elements across platforms enhance their brand's visibility and make a lasting impression.

3. The Rule of Seven:

• Fact: Consumers often need to encounter a brand message at least seven times before taking action.
• Insight: The "Rule of Seven" highlights the importance of repeated exposure in marketing. Crafting multi-touchpoint campaigns and maintaining a consistent brand narrative across various channels can significantly impact conversion rates.

4. The Impact of Social Proof:

• Fact: Over 90% of consumers are influenced by online reviews and social proof in their purchasing decisions.
• Insight: Social proof, including customer testimonials and reviews, wields immense influence. Incorporating social proof into marketing strategies can build trust, credibility, and sway consumer choices.

5. Mobile-First Reality:

• Fact: More than half of global internet traffic comes from mobile devices.
• Insight: The prevalence of mobile usage underscores the importance of optimizing marketing strategies for mobile platforms. Mobile-friendly websites, apps, and campaigns are essential for reaching and engaging today's audience effectively.

6. The Paradox of Choice:

• Fact: Offering too many choices can overwhelm consumers and lead to decision paralysis.
• Insight: Simplifying choices in marketing messages can enhance consumer decision-making. Marketers who strategically narrow down options can facilitate quicker and more confident choices from their audience.

7. The Impact of Storytelling on Memory:

• Fact: Information presented in the form of a story is up to 22 times more memorable than facts alone.
• Insight: Leveraging storytelling in marketing creates a powerful avenue for brand recall. Crafting narratives that resonate emotionally with the audience enhances message retention and brand affinity.

8. The Influence of Micro-Influencers:

• Fact: Micro-influencers often have higher engagement rates than macro-influencers.
• Insight: Collaborating with micro-influencers who have niche and highly engaged audiences can be more impactful than reaching out to larger, less-engaged audiences. Quality often trumps quantity in influencer marketing.

Unveiling these lesser-known facts about marketing offers a glimpse into the intricacies of consumer behavior, the power of psychological triggers, and the evolving landscape of effective marketing strategies. Armed with these insights, marketers can navigate the complexities of the industry with a more informed and strategic approach.

Dispelling Common Myths in the Field

In the ever-evolving landscape of marketing, certain myths and misconceptions persist, potentially hindering strategic decision-making. It's essential to dispel these myths and provide a clearer understanding of the realities shaping the industry. Here, we debunk some common myths:

1. Myth: "More Content Equals More Engagement":

    - Reality: Quality trumps quantity in content marketing.
    - Clarification: While consistency is important, flooding platforms with excessive content can lead to audience fatigue. Focus on creating valuable, relevant, and high-quality content that resonates with your target audience.

2. Myth: "Marketing is Only About Selling":

    - Reality: Effective marketing is about building relationships and providing value.
    - Clarification: Viewing marketing solely as a sales tool can alienate audiences. Successful marketing strategies prioritize customer relationships, trust-building, and delivering solutions that genuinely meet consumer needs.

3. Myth: "SEO is Only About Keywords":

    - Reality: SEO involves a holistic approach beyond keyword optimization.
    - Clarification: While keywords are essential, modern SEO encompasses user experience, content quality, site structure, and mobile optimization. A well-rounded SEO strategy considers various factors for sustainable organic growth.

4. Myth: "Email Marketing is Outdated":

    - Reality: Email marketing remains a potent tool for engagement and conversions.
    - Clarification: Far from being outdated, email marketing continues to deliver impressive ROI. Personalized and targeted email campaigns can nurture leads, retain customers, and drive meaningful interactions.

5. Myth: "Social Media is Only for Business to Customer [B2C]":

   - Reality: Social media is valuable for both B2C and B2B [Business to Business] marketing.
   - Clarification: Regardless of business type, social media platforms offer opportunities for brand visibility, thought leadership, and community building. B2B companies can leverage social media to connect with industry professionals and showcase expertise.

6. Myth: "Marketing Automation is Set-and-Forget":

   - Reality: Effective marketing automation requires ongoing optimization and monitoring.
   - Clarification: While automation streamlines processes, it's not a hands-off solution. Regularly review and refine automated workflows to ensure they align with evolving marketing goals and maintain relevance.

7. Myth: "Big Budgets Guarantee Successful Campaigns":

   - Reality: Creativity and strategy often matter more than budget size.
   - Clarification: While a budget provides resources, creative thinking and strategic execution play pivotal roles. Many successful campaigns have thrived on ingenuity and resonant messaging rather than extensive financial investments.

8. Myth: "Marketing is Exclusively Digital":

   - Reality: An integrated approach involving both digital and traditional channels can be powerful.
   - Clarification: While digital marketing is crucial, integrating it with traditional methods like print, events, and direct mail can create a comprehensive strategy. The most effective campaigns often utilize a blend of online and offline channels.

By dispelling these common myths, marketers can navigate the industry with a more accurate understanding of what truly drives success. Embracing these realities allows for strategic decision-making, fostering innovation and adaptability in an ever-changing marketing landscape.

Chapter 12

QUOTABLE WISDOM: BEST QUOTES ABOUT MARKETING

Compiling Inspirational and Thought-Provoking Quotes

In the ever-evolving realm of marketing, the wisdom distilled in succinct quotes can serve as guiding lights, offering insights from industry leaders, thinkers, and visionaries. Here, we compile a collection of inspirational and thought-provoking quotes that encapsulate the essence of marketing:

1. "The best marketing doesn't feel like marketing." — Tom Fishburne

Insight: This quote by Tom Fishburne emphasizes the importance of creating authentic and engaging experiences for the audience. Successful marketing seamlessly integrates into the consumer's life, feeling more like a valuable interaction than a sales pitch.

2. "People don't buy what you do; they buy why you do it." — Simon Sinek

Insight: Simon Sinek's quote underscores the significance of communicating the purpose and values behind a brand. By understanding and aligning with a brand's 'why,' consumers are more likely to connect on a deeper level.

3. "Content is fire, social media is gasoline." — Jay Baer

Insight: Jay Baer's metaphor captures the dynamic relationship between content and social media. Compelling content serves as the core, while social media amplifies its reach and impact.

4. "Your brand is a story unfolding across all customer touchpoints." — Jonah Sachs

Insight: Jonah Sachs reminds us that a brand is not just a logo or product; it's a narrative. Every interaction contributes to the unfolding story that shapes consumer perceptions.

5. "The consumer is not a moron, she's your wife." — David Ogilvy

Insight: David Ogilvy's quote emphasizes the importance of respecting and understanding the intelligence of the consumer. Successful marketing recognizes the audience as informed and discerning individuals.

6. "The aim of marketing is to know and understand the customer so well, the product or service fits them and sells itself." — Peter Drucker

Insight: Peter Drucker's quote highlights the fundamental principle of customer-centric marketing. Truly understanding the customer leads to products and services that naturally resonate and meet their needs.

7. "Don't be afraid to get creative and experiment with your marketing." — Mike Volpe

Insight: Mike Volpe encourages marketers to embrace creativity and experimentation. In the ever-evolving landscape, innovation is key to staying relevant and capturing audience attention.

8. "The best way to predict the future is to create it." — Peter Drucker

Insight: Peter Drucker's wisdom encourages a proactive approach. In marketing, anticipating and adapting to changes ensures a brand's ability to shape its own path in the future.

9. "The man who stops marketing to save money is like the man who stops a clock to save time." — Henry Ford

Insight: Henry Ford's quote vividly illustrates the folly of discontinuing marketing efforts for the sake of cost-saving. It emphasizes the ongoing nature of marketing as a vital investment.

10. "Good marketing makes the company look smart. Great marketing makes the customer feel smart." — Joe Chernov

Insight: Joe Chernov's quote highlights the transformative power of great marketing, emphasizing the importance of empowering customers and creating experiences that resonate with their intelligence.

These quotes encapsulate timeless principles and contemporary insights that resonate in the marketing world. They serve as beacons of inspiration, guiding marketers in their quest to create impactful and meaningful connections with their audience.

Insights from Industry Leaders and Visionaries

Gleaning insights from those who have navigated the marketing landscape successfully offers invaluable perspectives for aspiring marketers and seasoned professionals alike. Here, we present a compilation of direct quotes from industry leaders and visionaries that provide unique insights into the art and science of marketing:

1. "In marketing, I've seen only one strategy that can't miss — and that is to market to your best customers first, your best prospects second and the rest of the world last." — John Romero

Perspective: John Romero emphasizes the strategic importance of prioritizing existing customers and ideal prospects. This targeted approach ensures focused efforts and cultivates loyalty.

2. "Don't find customers for your products, find products for your customers." — Seth Godin

Perspective: Seth Godin's quote underscores the significance of aligning products with customer needs. Successful marketing begins with understanding and addressing the genuine requirements of the audience.

3. "The best marketing doesn't just focus on the sale; it focuses on building relationships with the audience. Sales may follow, but loyalty endures." — Ann Handley

Perspective: Ann Handley highlights the enduring value of relationship-focused marketing. Building connections with the audience fosters long-term loyalty that extends beyond individual transactions.

4. "The consumer isn't a moron; she's your wife. You insult her intelligence if you assume that a mere slogan and a few vapid adjectives will persuade her to buy anything." — David Ogilvy

Perspective: David Ogilvy's quote reiterates the importance of respecting the intelligence of the consumer. Effective marketing engages with sincerity and substance.

5. "Your culture is your brand." — Tony Hsieh

Perspective: Tony Hsieh emphasizes the interconnectedness of organizational culture and brand identity. A positive internal culture radiates outward, shaping the perception of the brand.

6. "Don't be afraid to get creative and experiment with your marketing." — Mike Volpe

Perspective: Mike Volpe's encouragement to embrace creativity and experimentation echoes the need for innovation and adaptability in the ever-evolving marketing landscape.

7. "Content builds relationships. Relationships are built on trust. Trust drives revenue." — Andrew Davis

Perspective: Andrew Davis underscores the pivotal role of trust in driving revenue. Building meaningful relationships through content establishes a foundation for sustained success.

8. "Branding is not about the stuff you make, but the stories you tell." — Seth Godin

Perspective: Seth Godin's second inclusion emphasizes the narrative aspect of branding. Crafting compelling stories resonates more deeply with audiences than focusing solely on products.

9. "Marketing's job is never done. It's about perpetual motion. We must continue to innovate every day." — Beth Comstock

Perspective: Beth Comstock highlights the dynamic and ever-evolving nature of marketing. A commitment to perpetual innovation is essential for staying relevant in the fast-paced industry.

10. "Your most unhappy customers are your greatest source of learning." — Bill Gates

Perspective: Bill Gates emphasizes the importance of learning from customer feedback, even when it's critical. Adapting based on customer experiences contributes to continuous improvement and success.

These insights from industry leaders and visionaries offer a diverse range of perspectives, each contributing to the rich tapestry of marketing wisdom. By delving into the thoughts of these influencers, marketers gain valuable lessons to inform their strategies and navigate the complexities of the marketing landscape.

Chapter 13

LEGENDARY FIGURES: ICONS OF THE MARKETING WORLD

Profiles of Influential Marketing Personalities

Delving into the lives and accomplishments of legendary figures in the marketing world provides a glimpse into the individuals who have shaped the industry. Here, we present concise profiles of influential marketing personalities whose innovative thinking and groundbreaking contributions have left an indelible mark:

1. David Ogilvy: The Father of Advertising

   Background: David Ogilvy, often referred to as the "Father of Advertising," founded Ogilvy & Mather and became a pioneer in the industry during the mid-20th century. •

   Legacy: Known for his iconic campaigns and principles like "The consumer isn't a moron; she's your wife," Ogilvy's legacy lies in his emphasis on research, creativity, and the power of compelling storytelling.

2. Jacki Kelley: Visionary Architect of Global Media Excellence

   Background: Jacki Kelley, the Global CEO at Universal McCann, brings a wealth of experience to her role, having held key positions in leading advertising and media agencies. With a background that includes roles at Bloomberg Media and Dentsu Aegis Network, she has consistently demonstrated expertise in navigating the complexities of the media and marketing landscape.

   Legacy: As a dynamic leader, Kelley has steered Universal McCann to new heights, reshaping the agency's approach to media and communication. Her visionary strategies have not only elevated the agency's global presence but have also set industry benchmarks. Under her leadership, Universal McCann continues to be a trailblazer, pushing boundaries in the ever-evolving world of media and advertising.

3. Seth Godin: Modern Marketing Maven

   Background: Seth Godin is a prolific author, speaker, and entrepreneur known for his insights into modern marketing. He's authored several influential books, including "Purple Cow" and "Permission Marketing."

   Legacy: Godin's impact lies in his ability to foresee marketing trends, emphasizing permission, authenticity, and the need for remarkable, standout ideas in a crowded marketplace.

4. Coco Chanel: Fashion Icon and Marketing Innovator

   Background: Coco Chanel, a legendary fashion designer, revolutionized the industry by creating a brand that represented elegance and simplicity.

   Legacy: Chanel's marketing genius lies in her ability to create a timeless brand associated with sophistication and freedom. Her iconic designs and innovative marketing strategies continue to influence the fashion world.

5. Leo Burnett: Advertising Trailblazer

   Background: Leo Burnett was a renowned advertising executive who founded the Leo Burnett Company in 1935. He was a creative force behind memorable campaigns like the Marlboro Man and the Jolly Green Giant.

   Legacy: Burnett's legacy is deeply rooted in creativity and creating advertising that resonates emotionally. His agency's focus on storytelling and human connection remains influential in the industry.

6. Philip Kotler: The Marketing Guru

   Background: Philip Kotler is an influential marketing author and professor. His books, including "Marketing Management," have become foundational texts in the field.

   Legacy: Kotler's contributions to marketing education and thought leadership have shaped the discipline. His insights into consumer behavior, segmentation, and strategic marketing continue to guide marketers worldwide.

7. Tiger Savage: Creative Maverick and Visionary Leader in Modern Advertising

   Background: Tiger Savage is a distinguished figure in advertising, recognized for her role as a creative force and industry leader. With an extensive background in advertising agencies like Droga5 and Chiat/Day, Savage has been instrumental in shaping compelling brand narratives.

   Legacy: Savage's impact on advertising is marked by her fearless approach to creativity. She has consistently pushed boundaries, leaving an imprint on memorable campaigns. As a trailblazer, she challenges conventional norms, contributing to the evolution of modern advertising and inspiring a new generation of creatives.

8. Kotler's Collaborator: Gary Armstrong

   Background: Gary Armstrong is an esteemed marketing professor, co-authoring several influential textbooks, including "Principles of Marketing," with Philip Kotler.

   Legacy: Armstrong's collaborative work with Kotler has had a profound impact on marketing education globally. Their textbooks are widely used, providing students with comprehensive insights into marketing principles.

9. Jagdish Sheth: Renowned Marketing Scholar

   Background: Jagdish Sheth is a distinguished marketing scholar and professor known for his groundbreaking work in consumer behavior, relationship marketing, and competitive strategy.

   Legacy: Sheth's contributions to marketing theory and academia have earned him international acclaim. His research has advanced understanding in areas crucial to strategic marketing and consumer insights.

10. Shelly Lazarus: Advertising Trailblazer

    Background: Shelly Lazarus served as the Chairman and CEO of Ogilvy & Mather, one of the world's leading advertising agencies. She played a pivotal role in shaping the agency's creative direction.

    Legacy: Lazarus is renowned for her leadership in the advertising industry, breaking barriers as a female executive. Her impact on branding and advertising strategies has been profound.

11. Neil Patel: Digital Marketing Expert

    Background: Neil Patel is a renowned digital marketing expert, entrepreneur, and author. He co-founded Crazy Egg, Hello Bar, and KISSmetrics.

    Legacy: Patel is a leading figure in digital marketing, sharing insights through his blog, speaking engagements, and consulting. His expertise in SEO, content marketing, and analytics has shaped modern online marketing strategies.

12. Anne Wojcicki: Pioneer in Healthcare Marketing

    Background: Anne Wojcicki is the co-founder and CEO of 23andMe, a direct-to-consumer genetic testing company. Her background includes healthcare marketing and biotechnology.

    Legacy: Wojcicki has transformed healthcare marketing by making genetic testing accessible to the public. Her innovative approach has influenced the intersection of marketing and personalized health.

13. George Lois: Advertising Creative Legend

    Background: George Lois is an iconic advertising creative director and designer. He is known for his innovative campaigns, including the legendary "I want my MTV" commercials.

    Legacy: Lois revolutionized advertising creativity, creating memorable campaigns that pushed boundaries. His impact on visual storytelling and brand messaging remains influential.

14. Mary Wells Lawrence: Pioneering Force in Marketing Innovation

    Background: Mary Wells Lawrence co-founded the Wells Rich Greene agency. She was the first female CEO of a company listed on the New York Stock Exchange, revolutionizing the industry in the Mad Men era.

    Legacy: Known for her innovative campaigns, Lawrence left an indelible mark on advertising. Her creative prowess and strategic thinking reshaped how brands approached marketing. As a pioneering woman in a male-dominated field, she paved the way for future generations of female leaders in advertising.

15. Jack Ma: E-Commerce Pioneer in Asia

    Background: Jack Ma is a Chinese entrepreneur and co-founder of Alibaba Group, a global e-commerce and technology conglomerate.

    Legacy: Ma's influence on e-commerce and digital marketing in Asia is profound. His leadership has shaped the evolution of online retail and technology marketing on a global scale.

16. Satoshi Nakamoto: Founder of Cryptocurrency and Blockchain

    Background: The mysterious figure behind the creation of Bitcoin and the concept of blockchain technology.

    Legacy: Nakamoto's white paper on Bitcoin laid the foundation for decentralized currency and blockchain technology, influencing the marketing landscape around cryptocurrency.

17. Ann Lewnes: Chief Marketing Officer at Adobe Systems

    Background: Ann Lewnes serves as the Chief Marketing Officer at Adobe Systems, leading the company's global marketing initiatives.

    Legacy: Lewnes has been instrumental in Adobe's marketing success, steering the brand's digital marketing efforts and contributing to the company's thought leadership in the tech industry.

18. Guy Kawasaki: Author and Evangelist

    Background: Guy Kawasaki is a marketing specialist, author, and former chief evangelist for Apple.

    Legacy: Kawasaki's books, including "The Art of the Start," have become influential guides for entrepreneurs. His insights into marketing, entrepreneurship, and innovation continue to shape the startup landscape.

19. Charlene Li: Author and Digital Marketing Expert

    Background: Charlene Li is an entrepreneur, author, and principal analyst at Altimeter, a Prophet Company.

    Legacy: Li's expertise in digital marketing and social media has made her a thought leader in the industry. Her books, such as "Groundswell" and "Open Leadership," provide valuable insights for marketers navigating the digital landscape.

20. Rory Sutherland: Behavioral Economics in Marketing

    Background: Rory Sutherland is a British advertising executive, author, and behavioral economics advocate.

    Legacy: Sutherland's work explores the intersection of psychology and marketing. As Vice Chairman of Ogilvy UK, his contributions to understanding consumer behavior and decision-making have left a lasting impact on marketing strategies.

21. Jesse Haines: Innovator at the Forefront of Mobile Advertising

   Background: Jesse Haines, Head of Marketing for Mobile Ads at Google, brings extensive expertise to her role, with a distinguished career in marketing and technology. With a background that includes pivotal roles in the tech industry, she has showcased a deep understanding of mobile advertising and its impact on the digital landscape.

   Legacy: As a strategic leader, Haines has played a transformative role in shaping Google's mobile advertising narrative. Her innovative approaches have positioned Google at the forefront of the industry, setting new standards for mobile marketing. Under her guidance, Google continues to redefine the mobile advertising landscape, embracing emerging trends and technologies.

22. Steve Jobs: Visionary Leader and Marketing Pioneer

   Background: Steve Jobs was the co-founder of Apple Inc. and a visionary entrepreneur known for his role in revolutionizing the tech industry.

   Legacy: Jobs had a profound impact on marketing, emphasizing sleek design, innovation, and the creation of a brand ecosystem. His product launches, including iconic devices like the iPhone, showcased a marketing approach that blended technology and consumer experience. Steve Jobs' influence extends beyond product development; his marketing philosophy and ability to create a brand that resonates with consumers have left an enduring mark on the marketing landscape.

These profiles offer glimpses into the lives and legacies of marketing personalities who have significantly shaped the industry. Each figure brings a unique perspective, leaving an enduring mark on marketing history.

Chapter 14

AGENCY SPOTLIGHT: THE OGILVY CASE STUDY

Exploring the History and Success Stories of Ogilvy

Delving into the legacy of Ogilvy & Mather unveils a narrative that intertwines creativity, strategy, and an unwavering commitment to excellence. This chapter explores the captivating journey of Ogilvy, a powerhouse in the advertising and marketing world, examining its history, defining moments, and the success stories that have made it an industry icon.

Founding Vision: The Birth of Ogilvy & Mather

David Ogilvy, often regarded as the "Father of Advertising," founded Ogilvy & Mather in 1948 with a vision grounded in research, honesty, and creativity. His principles, as outlined in his book "Confessions of an Advertising Man," laid the foundation for the agency's ethos.

Creative Excellence: Timeless Campaigns

Ogilvy's creative brilliance is evidenced by timeless campaigns that have etched themselves into the collective memory of consumers. The legendary "Dove Campaign for Real Beauty," "The Man in the Hathaway Shirt," and the iconic "Rolls-Royce Attracts the Right People" are just a glimpse of Ogilvy's transformative impact on advertising.

Global Expansion: Ogilvy's Reach Across Continents

Ogilvy's success is not confined to a single region. The agency strategically expanded its reach, establishing a global presence with offices spanning across continents. This expansion allowed Ogilvy to cater to diverse markets while maintaining its commitment to localized insights and cultural nuances.

Digital Evolution: Adapting to Changing Landscapes

In an era of digital transformation, Ogilvy has been at the forefront of adapting to changing marketing landscapes. The agency's innovative digital campaigns, such as

IBM's "Smarter Planet" and American Express's "Small Business Saturday," showcase Ogilvy's ability to seamlessly integrate traditional values with contemporary mediums.

Cultural Impact: Beyond Advertising

Ogilvy's influence extends beyond the realm of advertising. The agency has made significant contributions to marketing literature and thought leadership. David Ogilvy's writings, along with the agency's white papers and publications, continue to be essential readings for marketers and advertisers globally.

Awards and Accolades: Recognizing Excellence

Ogilvy's excellence has not gone unnoticed. The agency has been a recipient of numerous industry awards, celebrating its creativity, strategic insights, and overall impact on the marketing landscape. These accolades serve as a testament to Ogilvy's enduring commitment to excellence.

Leadership and Talent: Nurturing the Best

The agency's success can be attributed not only to its visionary founders but also to the talented individuals who have contributed to Ogilvy's legacy. The nurturing of creative minds, strategic thinkers, and marketing experts has been a hallmark of Ogilvy's approach to talent management.

Ogilvy Today: A Continuing Legacy

As Ogilvy & Mather transformed into Ogilvy, the agency continues to shape the future of marketing. With a renewed focus on collaboration, innovation, and customer-centric strategies, Ogilvy remains a dynamic force in the ever-evolving advertising and marketing landscape.

This subchapter concludes with a reflection on Ogilvy's enduring impact on the marketing industry. From its foundational principles to its evolution into a global marketing giant, Ogilvy's story serves as a source of inspiration and insight for marketers, advertisers, and enthusiasts alike.

Insights into Key Team Members and Their Impactful Campaigns

Unveiling the magic behind Ogilvy's success involves acknowledging the brilliance of its key team members. These individuals, with their innovative thinking and strategic prowess, have been the driving force behind some of Ogilvy's most impactful campaigns.

1. David Ogilvy: The Architect of Timeless Strategies

Contribution: As the founder, David Ogilvy laid the groundwork for Ogilvy's success. His timeless strategies, articulated in his writings, guided the agency to prioritize research, honesty, and creativity.

2. Bill Bernbach: A Collaborative Creative Force

Contribution: Bill Bernbach, though not a direct Ogilvy team member, was instrumental in influencing David Ogilvy. As a co-founder of DDB, he championed creativity and collaboration, principles echoed in Ogilvy's approach.

3. Charlotte Beers: Breaking Gender Barriers

Contribution: Charlotte Beers, Ogilvy's first female Vice President, shattered gender norms in the industry. Her impactful campaigns, including memorable work for Uncle Ben's and Head & Shoulders, showcased her strategic marketing brilliance.

4. Rory Sutherland: Behavioral Economics in Action

Contribution: Rory Sutherland, Vice Chairman of Ogilvy UK, brought behavioral economics into the spotlight. His campaigns emphasized the psychology of consumer behavior, showcasing the power of unconventional thinking.

5. Shelly Lazarus: Modernizing Branding for IBM

Contribution: Shelly Lazarus, former Chairman and CEO of Ogilvy & Mather, played a pivotal role in modernizing branding. Her campaigns, especially the rebranding of IBM, demonstrated her strategic leadership.

6. Tham Khai Meng: Crafting Stories for Coca-Cola

Contribution: Tham Khai Meng, former Chief Creative Officer, led Ogilvy's creative teams to new heights. His work on Coca-Cola campaigns exemplified a storytelling approach that resonated with global audiences.

7. Steve Harrison: Innovations in Direct Marketing

Contribution: Steve Harrison, former Global Creative Director, left an indelible mark on direct marketing. His campaigns, including those for American Express, showcased the power of personalized and impactful direct communication.

8. Annette King: Navigating the Digital Landscape

Contribution: Annette King, former CEO of Ogilvy UK, brought a digital focus to the agency. Her leadership saw Ogilvy adapting to the digital age, ensuring the agency's relevance in an evolving marketing landscape.

9. Brian Fetherstonhaugh: Global Leadership

Contribution: Brian Fetherstonhaugh, OgilvyOne's Chairman and CEO, contributed to Ogilvy's global success. His strategic leadership emphasized the importance of data-driven marketing and customer-centric approaches.

10. Thabo Sefolosha: Diversity and Inclusion Advocate

Contribution: Thabo Sefolosha, Ogilvy's Global Chief Diversity, Equity & Inclusion Officer, is championing diversity within the agency. His efforts are contributing to a more inclusive and innovative creative environment.

The collaborative brilliance of these key team members has left an enduring impact on Ogilvy's legacy. Their innovative campaigns not only shaped the agency's trajectory but also influenced the broader marketing landscape. Ogilvy's success is a testament to the collective genius of these creative minds.

Chapter 15

STRATEGIC PROWESS: COMPANIES WITH EXCEPTIONAL MARKETING STRATEGIES

Analyzing Successful Marketing Strategies Across Industries

In the dynamic landscape of marketing, certain companies stand out for their exceptional strategies that transcend industry boundaries. This subchapter delves into the core elements of successful marketing strategies employed by diverse businesses, offering valuable insights for marketers seeking inspiration and learning from the best.

1. Apple Inc.: The Art of Anticipation

Strategy: Apple's marketing prowess lies in creating anticipation. Through carefully orchestrated product launches, minimalist yet compelling advertising, and a focus on user experience, Apple captivates audiences, turning each product release into a global event.

2. Nike: Inspiring through Storytelling

Strategy: Nike's marketing goes beyond products; it's about stories. By aligning with inspiring athletes and weaving compelling narratives around sports and empowerment, Nike creates a brand that resonates emotionally, fostering strong connections with its audience.

3. Coca-Cola: Timeless Branding and Emotional Resonance

Strategy: Coca-Cola's timeless branding strategy focuses on emotional resonance. Through consistent messaging, iconic imagery, and global campaigns, Coca-Cola has successfully associated its brand with joy, celebration, and shared moments.

4. Google: User-Centric Innovation

Strategy: Google's success is rooted in user-centric innovation. By consistently delivering products and services that address user needs and simplify complex tasks, Google has become synonymous with online search, productivity, and technological advancement.

5. Amazon: Customer-Centric Everything

Strategy: Amazon's relentless commitment to customer-centricity sets it apart. From personalized recommendations to efficient delivery services, Amazon's marketing strategy revolves around enhancing the customer experience at every touchpoint, fostering loyalty and trust.

6. Airbnb: Community-Centric Brand Building

Strategy: Airbnb's success is built on community-centric brand building. Through user-generated content, authentic storytelling, and a focus on the unique experiences their platform offers, Airbnb has created a global community that transcends traditional hospitality marketing, and has successfully differentiated itself in the competitive travel industry.

7. Tesla: Disruptive Innovation and Cult Branding

Strategy: Tesla's marketing strategy is a blend of disruptive innovation and cult branding. By challenging industry norms, fostering a passionate community, and leveraging word-of-mouth marketing, Tesla has redefined the electric car market and beyond.

8. Patagonia: Sustainability as a Brand Pillar

Strategy: Patagonia's marketing strategy is rooted in environmental sustainability. By aligning its brand with eco-friendly practices, transparency, and a commitment to social responsibility, Patagonia has attracted a loyal customer base that shares its values.

9. Spotify: Personalization in the Streaming Era

Strategy: Spotify excels in personalization. Through data-driven algorithms, curated playlists, and personalized recommendations, Spotify's marketing strategy revolves around offering a tailored music experience, keeping users engaged and connected.

10. Netflix: Data-Driven Content Personalization

Strategy: Netflix's success lies in data-driven content personalization. By leveraging user data to recommend tailored content, investing in original productions, and creating binge-worthy series, Netflix has become a dominant force in the streaming industry.

11. Starbucks: Creating Experiential Spaces

Strategy: Starbucks excels in creating experiential spaces. Beyond selling coffee, Starbucks has crafted a unique atmosphere, emphasizing community, individualization, and a "third place" outside of home and work. Their marketing strategy focuses on the overall coffee experience.

12. Disney: Mastering the Art of Storytelling

Strategy: Disney's marketing strategy revolves around storytelling. Whether through animated classics, theme parks, or the acquisition of major franchises like Marvel and Star Wars, Disney continues to captivate audiences with timeless narratives and immersive experiences.

13. LVMH (Moët Hennessy Louis Vuitton): Luxury Branding Mastery

Strategy: LVMH's success lies in luxury branding mastery. With a portfolio including iconic brands like Louis Vuitton, Moët & Chandon, and Hennessy, LVMH's marketing strategy emphasizes exclusivity, craftsmanship, and storytelling to maintain an aura of luxury.

14. BMW: The Ultimate Driving Experience

Strategy: BMW's marketing strategy centers around the ultimate driving experience. By emphasizing performance, luxury, and innovative technology, BMW has created a brand synonymous with driving pleasure and engineering excellence.

15. Huawei: Global Tech Expansion

Strategy: Huawei's success is rooted in global tech expansion. By establishing itself as a leader in telecommunications and consumer electronics, Huawei's marketing strategy includes a focus on innovation, global partnerships, and building trust in its brand.

16. Red Bull: Branding Through Extreme Sports

Strategy: Red Bull's marketing strategy extends beyond energy drinks to extreme sports and content creation. Through sponsorships, events, and unique marketing stunts, Red Bull has cultivated a brand associated with excitement, adventure, and high-energy lifestyles.

17. Natura: Ethical Beauty and Sustainability

Strategy: Natura, a Brazilian beauty brand, emphasizes ethical beauty and sustainability. With a commitment to natural ingredients, environmental responsibility, and social impact, Natura's marketing strategy resonates with conscious consumers.

18. Toyota: Hybrid Innovation and Environmental Focus

Strategy: Toyota's marketing strategy focuses on hybrid innovation and environmental consciousness. By leading in the hybrid car market, emphasizing fuel efficiency, and promoting sustainability, Toyota has positioned itself as a leader in eco-friendly transportation.

19. Alibaba: E-Commerce Dominance in Asia

Strategy: Alibaba's success is rooted in e-commerce dominance in Asia. Through platforms like Alibaba and Taobao, the company has revolutionized online shopping, employing innovative strategies like Singles' Day to drive sales.

20. Manchester United: Global Sports Branding

Strategy: Manchester United's marketing strategy extends beyond sports to global branding. With a massive fan base, strategic partnerships, and a focus on digital engagement, the football club has created a brand that transcends borders.

21. Samsung: Innovation as a Differentiator

Strategy: Samsung's marketing strategy revolves around innovation as a differentiator. By consistently introducing cutting-edge technology and products, emphasizing sleek design, and investing in memorable advertising, Samsung has become a leader in the consumer electronics market.

22. Alibaba: E-Commerce Dominance in Asia

Strategy: Alibaba's success is rooted in e-commerce dominance in Asia. Through platforms like Alibaba and Taobao, the company has revolutionized online shopping, employing innovative strategies like Singles' Day to drive sales.

Lessons Learned from their Strategies and Execution: Learning from Companies with a Strong Marketing Game

In the dynamic landscape of marketing, certain companies shine as beacons of strategic prowess. This subchapter delves into valuable lessons and insights derived from companies that have consistently demonstrated a strong marketing game, offering a rich tapestry of inspiration for marketers and businesses seeking to elevate their marketing strategies.

1. Focus on Brand Storytelling: Nike

Lesson: Nike's success underscores the power of brand storytelling. By aligning with compelling narratives and inspirational figures, Nike has created an emotional connection with its audience, emphasizing that a brand's story is as essential as its products.

2. Customer-Centricity: Amazon

Lesson: Amazon's relentless focus on customer-centricity stands out. The e-commerce giant excels by prioritizing customer experience, personalized recommendations, and efficient service. This lesson underscores the importance of placing the customer at the center of marketing strategies.

3. Authenticity and Sustainability: Patagonia

Lesson: Patagonia's commitment to authenticity and sustainability serves as a beacon for purpose-driven marketing. By aligning with environmental causes and maintaining transparency, Patagonia has cultivated a loyal customer base, showcasing the impact of genuine brand values.

4. Innovation and Disruption: Tesla

Lesson: Tesla's marketing success is intertwined with innovation and disruption. The company redefined the automotive industry by emphasizing electric vehicles and cutting-edge technology. The lesson here is that marketing strategies should align with groundbreaking products or services.

5. Emotional Resonance: Coca-Cola

Lesson: Coca-Cola's timeless marketing teaches the importance of emotional resonance. Through consistent messaging, iconic visuals, and global campaigns, Coca-Cola has associated its brand with joy and shared moments, showcasing the enduring impact of emotional connections.

6. Digital Adaptation: Alibaba

Lesson: Alibaba's success in e-commerce highlights the necessity of digital adaptation. By leveraging technology, data analytics, and innovative strategies like Singles' Day, Alibaba showcases the transformative power of embracing digital trends in marketing.

7. Luxury Branding: LVMH (Moët Hennessy Louis Vuitton)

Lesson: LVMH's mastery in luxury branding teaches the importance of exclusivity and craftsmanship. The conglomerate's portfolio, including Louis Vuitton and Moët & Chandon, exemplifies how emphasizing luxury and storytelling can elevate a brand to iconic status.

8. Community Engagement: Airbnb

Lesson: Airbnb's success in community-centric brand building emphasizes the power of engagement. By fostering a sense of belonging, encouraging user-generated content, and emphasizing unique travel experiences, Airbnb demonstrates the impact of community-driven marketing.

9. Data-Driven Personalization: Spotify

Lesson: Spotify's strength in data-driven personalization illustrates the importance of customization. By leveraging user data for curated playlists and personalized recommendations, Spotify showcases the effectiveness of tailoring marketing efforts to individual preferences.

10. Global Sports Branding: Manchester United

Lesson: Manchester United's global sports branding teaches the significance of creating a brand that transcends borders. Through a massive fan base, strategic partnerships, and digital engagement, the football club showcases the global impact of effective sports marketing.

In summary, these lessons from industry giants provide a roadmap for marketing success. From Nike's storytelling prowess to Amazon's customer-centricity, each insight contributes to a holistic understanding of effective strategies.

By embracing innovation, authenticity, and community engagement, businesses can navigate the dynamic landscape, fostering enduring connections and staying ahead in the competitive realm of marketing.

Chapter 16

HOW BUDGET ALLOCATION CORRELATES WITH MARKETING SUCCESS

In the realm of substantial marketing budgets, the correlation between effective budget allocation and marketing success is a critical determinant of a company's ability to achieve its strategic goals. This subchapter delves into the nuanced strategies employed by companies with significant budgets, highlighting the key elements that contribute to marketing success.

1. Strategic Alignment with Business Goals: Procter & Gamble (P&G)

Approach: P&G strategically aligns its marketing budget with overarching business goals, ensuring that budget allocations support brand visibility, product launches, and market expansion.

Outcome: This alignment has contributed to P&G's success in maintaining a diverse portfolio of household brands with global reach.

2. Holistic Brand Building: Coca-Cola

Approach: Coca-Cola dedicates a substantial portion of its budget to holistic brand building, encompassing iconic campaigns, sponsorships, and continuous innovation.

Outcome: This holistic approach has fortified Coca-Cola's position as a cultural icon, showcasing how diversified budget allocations contribute to sustained brand resonance.

3. Innovation and Product Launches: Apple Inc.

Approach: Apple allocates a considerable budget to innovative product launches, marketing spectacles, and strategic brand positioning.

Outcome: This approach has fueled Apple's success, creating a cult-like following and establishing the company as a trendsetter in the tech industry.

4. Digital Dominance and User Engagement: Google

Approach: Google strategically allocates its marketing budget to reinforce digital dominance, focusing on user engagement, product launches, and search advertising.

Outcome: The result is evident in Google's continued dominance in online search and technology, showcasing the impact of targeted budget allocation.

5. Brand Reinvention: Microsoft

Approach: Microsoft utilizes a substantial marketing budget for brand reinvention, encompassing campaigns for diverse tech offerings and hardware products.

Outcome: Microsoft's strategic budget allocation has contributed to the company's evolving image, reflecting innovation and relevance in the tech landscape.

6. Social Media Dominance and Platform Expansion: Facebook

Approach: Facebook directs its marketing budget towards reinforcing social media dominance, user engagement, and platform expansion through advertising initiatives.

Outcome: This strategic allocation contributes to Facebook's continued global dominance in the social media landscape.

7. Automotive Innovation and Sustainability: Toyota

Approach: Toyota allocates its marketing budget to highlight automotive innovation, sustainability initiatives, and global presence.

Outcome: This approach has contributed to Toyota's success in maintaining a competitive edge in the automotive market.

8. Diverse Consumer Brands and Sustainable Messaging: Unilever

Approach: Unilever strategically allocates its marketing budget to communicate sustainable messaging, product innovation, and global campaigns for diverse consumer brands.

Outcome: This strategic alignment contributes to Unilever's success in catering to conscious consumers and maintaining a diverse product portfolio.

9. E-Commerce Dominance and Prime Impact: Amazon

Approach: Amazon allocates a substantial budget to maintain its e-commerce dominance, support Prime memberships, and drive advertising initiatives.

Outcome: This strategic approach reinforces Amazon's position as a global online marketplace and contributes to its sustained growth.

10. Global Sports Branding: Manchester United

Approach: Manchester United strategically allocates its marketing budget to reinforce global sports branding through fan engagement, strategic partnerships, and digital initiatives.

Outcome: This approach has solidified Manchester United's position as a global sports brand, showcasing the impact of strategic budget allocation.

TikTok Triumph: Mastering the Art of Strategic Marketing Budget Allocation

In the realm of substantial marketing budgets, it's essential to examine how companies strategically allocate their resources for optimal marketing success. This subchapter delves into the nuanced strategies employed by a diverse range of companies, including TikTok, highlighting the key elements that contribute to marketing success.

1. Strategic Alignment with User Engagement: TikTok

Approach: TikTok strategically allocates its marketing budget to enhance user engagement, content creation initiatives, and collaborations with influencers.

Outcome: This strategic alignment has contributed to TikTok's rapid rise, creating a global platform for short-form video content and establishing itself as a dominant force in the social media landscape.

2. Innovative Advertising Campaigns: TikTok

Approach: TikTok invests in innovative advertising campaigns, leveraging the platform's unique features to create engaging and interactive content.

Outcome: This approach has strengthened TikTok's appeal to both users and advertisers, showcasing the impact of innovative budget allocation in the competitive social media space.

3. Global Expansion and Partnerships: TikTok

Approach: TikTok strategically allocates budget for global expansion, forming partnerships with influencers, celebrities, and brands worldwide.

Outcome: This strategic move has propelled TikTok into an international phenomenon, demonstrating the power of global budget allocation for a social media platform.

4. Community Building and Trends: TikTok

Approach: TikTok directs its marketing budget towards fostering community building and embracing emerging trends through challenges and campaigns.

Outcome: This strategic allocation contributes to TikTok's reputation as a platform that thrives on creativity, authenticity, and community engagement.

5. Branding and User Acquisition: TikTok

Approach: TikTok strategically allocates budget to enhance branding efforts and acquire new users, focusing on creating a distinct identity in the crowded social media landscape.

Outcome: This strategic branding has played a pivotal role in TikTok's ability to attract diverse audiences and maintain its status as a leading social media platform.

As we examine how budget allocation correlates with marketing success, TikTok emerges as a compelling case study. By strategically allocating resources for user engagement, innovative campaigns, global expansion, community building, and branding, TikTok exemplifies the dynamic landscape of social media marketing. The platform's success underscores the importance of adaptability, creativity, and precision in budget allocation for optimal marketing outcomes.

In the intricate dance between budget allocation and marketing success, companies with substantial marketing budgets exemplify the art of strategic allocation. Whether aligning with business goals, emphasizing holistic brand building, fueling innovation, or dominating digital spaces, the correlation between where companies allocate their marketing budgets and the resulting success is a testament to the precision and foresight that define marketing excellence on a grand scale.

Financial Frontiers: Companies with the Biggest Marketing Budgets

A Deep Dive into Companies with Substantial Marketing Budgets

This chapter takes an in-depth exploration into the world of companies that command some of the most substantial marketing budgets. As financial powerhouses, these organizations wield significant resources to orchestrate campaigns, build brand presence, and dominate markets. Let's uncover the strategies, campaigns, and impacts of companies that invest heavily in their marketing endeavors.

1. Procter & Gamble (P&G): Household Brands and Global Reach

Overview: Procter & Gamble, a consumer goods giant, consistently boasts one of the most substantial marketing budgets globally.

Strategies: P&G allocates its budget strategically across diverse brands, emphasizing global reach and innovative advertising campaigns for products ranging from Tide to Pampers.

2. Coca-Cola: Iconic Branding and Sponsorships

Overview: Coca-Cola, a global beverage leader, is synonymous with iconic branding and a significant marketing budget.

Strategies: Coca-Cola's budget supports memorable campaigns, sponsorships of major events like the Olympics and FIFA World Cup, and continuous innovation to maintain its status as a cultural phenomenon.

3. Samsung: Cutting-Edge Technology and Global Presence

Overview: Samsung, a technology giant, dedicates substantial resources to its marketing endeavors.

Strategies: Samsung's marketing budget fuels campaigns highlighting cutting-edge technology, global partnerships, and innovative product launches, ensuring a strong brand presence in the competitive consumer electronics market.

4. Amazon: E-Commerce Dominance and Prime Impact

Overview: Amazon, the e-commerce behemoth, allocates a significant marketing budget to maintain its dominance.

Strategies: Amazon's marketing budget supports a range of initiatives, from Prime memberships to advertising campaigns, reinforcing its position as the go-to online marketplace.

5. Apple Inc.: Product Launch Spectacles and Brand Loyalty

Overview: Apple, renowned for its innovation, commands a substantial marketing budget for its product launches and brand-building efforts.

Strategies: Apple's marketing budget is strategically invested in creating product launch spectacles, fostering brand loyalty, and maintaining its premium positioning in the tech industry.

6. Google: Digital Dominance and Search Advertising

Overview: Google, a tech giant, utilizes a considerable marketing budget to reinforce its digital dominance.

Strategies: Google's budget supports search advertising, product launches, and initiatives that reinforce its position as a leader in the online search and technology space.

7. Microsoft: Diverse Tech Offerings and Brand Reinvention

Overview: Microsoft, with a diversified tech portfolio, allocates a substantial marketing budget for brand reinvention.

Strategies: Microsoft's marketing efforts encompass a broad range, from promoting software solutions to hardware products, reflecting the company's evolution and innovation.

8. Facebook: Social Media Dominance and User Engagement

Overview: Facebook, a social media giant, commands a substantial marketing budget for user engagement and platform expansion.

Strategies: Facebook's budget fuels advertising initiatives, platform enhancements, and acquisitions, contributing to its dominance in the global social media landscape.

9. Toyota: Automotive Innovation and Global Presence

Overview: Toyota, a leading automaker, allocates a substantial marketing budget to maintain its position in the automotive industry.

Strategies: Toyota's marketing budget supports campaigns highlighting innovation, sustainability, and global initiatives to solidify its standing in the competitive automotive market.

10. Unilever: Diverse Consumer Brands and Sustainable Messaging

Overview: Unilever, a consumer goods conglomerate, dedicates significant resources to market its diverse brand portfolio.

Strategies: Unilever's marketing budget focuses on sustainable messaging, product innovation, and global campaigns for household brands like Dove, Knorr, and Ben & Jerry's.

As we embark on a deep dive into the companies with the biggest marketing budgets, a common theme emerges—strategic allocation, global reach, innovation, and brand building. The substantial marketing budgets wielded by these companies serve as a testament to the integral role marketing plays in maintaining and expanding their market dominance.

Chapter 17

CAMPAIGN CHRONICLES: BEST MARKETING CAMPAIGNS CASE STUDIES

In-Depth Analyses of Renowned Marketing Campaigns

In this chapter, we embark on a journey through the intricate tapestry of marketing excellence by dissecting and analyzing some of the most renowned campaigns that have left an indelible mark on the industry. These case studies offer invaluable insights into the strategies, creativity, and execution that propelled these campaigns to success.

1. Nike's "Just Do It" Campaign

Background: Nike's iconic "Just Do It" campaign is a masterclass in motivational marketing.

Strategies: The campaign emphasized empowering messages, celebrity endorsements (such as Michael Jordan), and a focus on the spirit of athleticism.

Outcomes: "Just Do It" became a rallying cry, solidifying Nike's position as a brand synonymous with determination and achievement.

2. Apple's "Get a Mac" Campaign

Background: Apple's "Get a Mac" campaign is a classic example of comparative advertising.

Strategies: The campaign personified a Mac and a PC, highlighting the simplicity and innovation of the Mac.

Outcomes: "Get a Mac" reinforced Apple's brand identity, emphasizing the user-friendly and innovative aspects of its products.

3. Old Spice's "The Man Your Man Could Smell Like"

Background: Old Spice's humorous and memorable campaign aimed to redefine its image.

Strategies: The campaign featured a charismatic character, witty scripts, and interactive social media engagement.

Outcomes: Old Spice successfully rebranded itself, achieving increased sales and widespread cultural impact.

4. Dove's "Real Beauty" Campaign

Background: Dove's "Real Beauty" campaign challenged conventional beauty standards.

Strategies: The campaign featured real women, promoting body positivity and self-acceptance.

Outcomes: Dove's commitment to authenticity resonated, resulting in positive brand perception and increased sales.

5. Burger King's "Whopper Detour"

Background: Burger King's "Whopper Detour" campaign leveraged geolocation technology.

Strategies: The campaign encouraged customers to visit McDonald's locations to unlock a special deal on the Burger King app.

Outcomes: "Whopper Detour" generated buzz, showcasing the power of innovative marketing stunts.

6. ALS Ice Bucket Challenge

Background: The ALS Ice Bucket Challenge became a viral phenomenon for a charitable cause.

Strategies: Participants shared videos of themselves taking the challenge, raising awareness and donations for ALS research.

Outcomes: The campaign went viral globally, raising millions for ALS research and demonstrating the potential of user-generated content for a cause.

7. Red Bull's Stratos Space Jump

Background: Red Bull's Stratos Space Jump was a daring and high-profile stunt.

Strategies: The campaign involved Felix Baumgartner's freefall from the stratosphere, showcasing extreme sports and Red Bull's association with daring feats.

Outcomes: The Stratos Space Jump generated immense brand visibility, aligning Red Bull with adrenaline-fueled adventures.

8. Share a Coke Campaign by Coca-Cola

Background: Coca-Cola's "Share a Coke" campaign personalized its iconic bottles.

Strategies: Customizing bottles with popular names encouraged consumers to share and connect.

Outcomes: The campaign boosted engagement, personalizing the brand and increasing sales.

9. Oreo's "Dunk in the Dark" during Super Bowl

Background: Oreo's real-time marketing during a blackout at the Super Bowl became an instant hit.

Strategies: The brand quickly tweeted a clever message, showcasing the power of agility in social media.

Outcomes: Oreo's quick-witted response went viral, highlighting the impact of real-time marketing.

10. Heineken's "Worlds Apart" Social Experiment

Background: Heineken's "Worlds Apart" campaign brought people with opposing views together.

Strategies: The campaign focused on common ground and open conversation.

Outcomes: "Worlds Apart" fostered dialogue and positive brand perception, showcasing the impact of socially conscious marketing.

As we dissect these case studies, patterns of success emerge—whether through emotional storytelling, innovative stunts, real-time marketing, or socially conscious campaigns. Each case study represents a unique facet of marketing brilliance, offering valuable lessons and inspiration for marketers navigating the ever-evolving landscape.

Lessons Learned from Their Strategies and Execution

As we reflect on the in-depth analyses of renowned marketing campaigns, a wealth of lessons emerges from the strategies and executions that propelled these campaigns to success. Let's distill these invaluable insights, offering a guide for marketers eager to elevate their own campaigns.

1. Authentic Storytelling Resonates: Nike's "Just Do It" Campaign

Lesson: Nike's success lies in the authenticity of its storytelling. Brands should craft narratives that resonate with the audience's emotions, values, and aspirations.

2. Effective Comparative Advertising: Apple's "Get a Mac" Campaign

Lesson: Comparative advertising can be a powerful tool when executed effectively. Highlighting your product's strengths in contrast to competitors can solidify your brand positioning.

3. Humor and Memorable Characters: Old Spice's Campaign

Lesson: Humor, combined with memorable characters, can leave a lasting impression. A touch of wit and engaging personalities can elevate a brand's identity.

4. Challenging Beauty Standards: Dove's "Real Beauty" Campaign

Lesson: Challenging societal norms can create a strong connection with consumers. Authenticity in addressing real-world issues fosters trust and brand loyalty.

5. Innovative Marketing Stunts: Burger King's "Whopper Detour"

Lesson: Innovation and creativity in marketing stunts can capture attention and generate buzz. Thinking outside the box can set your brand apart.

6. User-Generated Content for Social Impact: ALS Ice Bucket Challenge

Lesson: Harnessing the power of user-generated content for a cause can create a viral movement. Encourage participation and align campaigns with meaningful purposes.

7. Extreme Sports and Brand Associations: Red Bull's Stratos Space Jump

Lesson: Associating your brand with daring feats and extreme sports can cultivate an adventurous and energetic brand image.

8. Personalization Boosts Engagement: Coca-Cola's "Share a Coke"

Lesson: Personalizing products can boost engagement. Creating a personalized connection with consumers enhances brand loyalty.

9. Real-Time Marketing Agility: Oreo's "Dunk in the Dark"

Lesson: Real-time marketing requires agility and quick-wittedness. Brands should be ready to capitalize on unexpected opportunities.

10. Socially Conscious Branding: Heineken's "Worlds Apart"

Lesson: Socially conscious campaigns that foster dialogue can create a positive brand perception. Aligning your brand with societal values can build trust.

The lessons learned from these campaigns form a blueprint for marketing brilliance. Whether it's the power of authentic storytelling, the impact of humor and memorable characters, or the effectiveness of innovative stunts, each campaign provides a unique lesson that can be applied across diverse industries and marketing landscapes. By understanding and implementing these insights, marketers can chart a course towards creating impactful and memorable campaigns that resonate with audiences globally.

Chapter 18

RESOURCES FOR CONTINUOUS LEARNING AND PROFESSIONAL DEVELOPMENT

Continuous learning is pivotal for staying ahead in the dynamic field of marketing. Here are resources that facilitate ongoing growth and development:

1. Marketing Blogs and Websites:

a. HubSpot Blog:

Why Follow: HubSpot's blog covers a wide range of marketing topics, providing insights into the latest trends, strategies, and industry updates.

b. Moz Blog:

Why Follow: Moz is a go-to resource for SEO enthusiasts. Their blog offers in-depth articles and guides on search engine optimization.

c. MarketingProfs:

Why Follow: MarketingProfs is a comprehensive platform offering marketing resources, articles, and webinars for professionals at every career stage.

2. Online Courses and Certifications:

a. Google Analytics Academy:

Why Enroll: Deepen your understanding of web analytics with Google Analytics Academy. Courses cover various aspects, from beginner to advanced levels.

b. Facebook Blueprint:

Why Enroll: Facebook Blueprint provides courses on advertising strategies across Facebook and Instagram, helping marketers stay adept with the latest advertising tools.

c. Coursera Specializations:

Why Enroll: Explore marketing specializations on Coursera from top universities and institutions worldwide. These programs offer a comprehensive curriculum to hone specific skills.

3. Podcasts for Marketing Insights:

a. "The Tim Ferriss Show" by Tim Ferriss:

Why Listen: Tim Ferriss interviews successful individuals across various fields, extracting valuable insights and strategies applicable to marketing and entrepreneurship.

b. "The Social Media Examiner Show" by Michael Stelzner:

Why Listen: Stay updated on social media trends and strategies with this podcast, featuring expert interviews and actionable tips.

c. "Marketing Over Coffee" by John Wall and Christopher Penn:

Why Listen: A casual, conversational podcast covering a variety of marketing topics, offering insights in a digestible format.

4. Professional Associations and Networking:

a. American Marketing Association (AMA):

Why Join: The AMA provides access to industry insights, events, and a network of marketing professionals. Membership fosters continuous learning and collaboration.

b. Digital Marketing Institute (DMI):

Why Join: DMI offers certifications and resources to advance your digital marketing skills. Membership provides exclusive access to industry updates and networking opportunities.

5. Industry Conferences and Events:

a. INBOUND by HubSpot:

Why Attend: INBOUND is a premier marketing conference offering keynotes, workshops, and networking opportunities. Stay informed about the latest marketing trends and innovations.

b. Content Marketing World:

Why Attend: This conference focuses on content marketing strategies, featuring expert speakers and workshops to enhance your content creation skills.

In the ever-evolving landscape of marketing, fostering a growth mindset is crucial. These resources provide continuous learning opportunities, ensuring that marketers stay informed, inspired, and equipped to navigate the challenges and seize the opportunities in this dynamic field.

Chapter 19

DATA-DRIVEN INSIGHTS: RESEARCH FINDINGS IN THE WORLD OF MARKETING

Presenting Key Research Data and Findings in Marketing

In the realm of marketing, leveraging data-driven insights is essential for making informed decisions and crafting effective strategies. This subchapter highlights key research data and findings that shed light on various facets of the marketing landscape.

1. Consumer Behavior Studies:

- a. E-Commerce Trends:

- Key Findings: Explore the latest trends in e-commerce, including consumer preferences, shopping habits, and the impact of emerging technologies.
- Implications for Marketers: Understand how e-commerce trends shape customer expectations, enabling marketers to tailor strategies for optimal engagement.

- b. Mobile Usage Patterns:

- Key Findings: Dive into research on mobile device usage, app preferences, and the role of mobile in the customer journey.
- Implications for Marketers: Craft mobile-friendly campaigns and optimize user experiences based on insights into mobile usage patterns.

2. Social Media Analytics:

- a. Effectiveness of Video Content:

- Key Findings: Uncover research insights into the effectiveness of video content on various social media platforms.
- Implications for Marketers: Tailor social media strategies to harness the power of video content for increased engagement and brand visibility.

- b. Influence of User-Generated Content:

- Key Findings: Examine the impact of user-generated content on brand perception and customer trust across social media channels.
- Implications for Marketers: Incorporate user-generated content strategies to build authenticity and foster community engagement.

3. Digital Advertising Trends:

- a. Effectiveness of Personalized Ads:

- Key Findings: Explore research on the effectiveness of personalized advertising in capturing audience attention and driving conversions.
- Implications for Marketers: Fine-tune personalized ad strategies to enhance relevance and resonate with target audiences.

- b. Ad Blocker Usage and Attitudes:

- Key Findings: Gain insights into consumer attitudes toward ad blockers and the factors influencing their adoption.
- Implications for Marketers: Develop strategies to navigate ad blocker challenges and create compelling, non-intrusive ad experiences.

4. Content Marketing Insights:

- a. Long-Form vs. Short-Form Content:

- Key Findings: Examine research comparing the effectiveness of long-form and short-form content in engaging audiences and driving conversions.
- Implications for Marketers: Tailor content strategies based on the preferred content length for specific target audiences.

- b. Content Consumption Across Channels:

- Key Findings: Understand how audiences consume content across various channels and devices.

- Implications for Marketers: Optimize content distribution strategies to align with the preferences and behaviors of diverse audiences.

By presenting and dissecting these key research findings, marketers can transform raw data into actionable insights. Armed with a deep understanding of consumer behaviors, social media dynamics, digital advertising trends, and content preferences, marketers can craft strategies that resonate with their target audiences and drive meaningful results in the ever-evolving landscape of marketing.

Implications for Decision-Making and Strategy Formulation

The wealth of research data and findings in marketing not only informs our understanding of consumer behaviors, social media dynamics, digital advertising trends, and content preferences but also holds profound implications for decision-making and strategy formulation. Here's a detailed examination of how these insights translate into actionable strategies:

1. Consumer Behavior Studies:

- a. E-Commerce Trends:

Decision-Making Implications: Marketers should prioritize online shopping experiences, streamline the checkout process, and leverage emerging technologies like augmented reality to enhance the overall e-commerce journey.

Strategic Formulation: Develop strategies that align with the growing trend of online shopping, focusing on personalized experiences and innovative technologies to gain a competitive edge.

- b. Mobile Usage Patterns:

Decision-Making Implications: With a significant portion of users accessing content via mobile devices, marketers should prioritize mobile-friendly campaigns, considering factors such as app preferences and device usage patterns.

Strategic Formulation: Craft strategies that optimize content for mobile, including mobile-responsive websites, app experiences, and mobile-centric advertising.

2. Social Media Analytics:

- a. Effectiveness of Video Content:

Decision-Making Implications: Recognizing the effectiveness of video content, marketers should allocate resources to produce engaging videos tailored to each platform's specifications.

Strategic Formulation: Develop a comprehensive video content strategy, focusing on storytelling, authenticity, and shareability to enhance brand visibility.

- b. Influence of User-Generated Content:

Decision-Making Implications: Acknowledging the impact of user-generated content, marketers should actively encourage and incorporate user-generated content into their campaigns.

Strategic Formulation: Formulate strategies that foster user-generated content, building brand authenticity and strengthening community connections.

3. Digital Advertising Trends:

- a. Effectiveness of Personalized Ads:

Decision-Making Implications: Given the effectiveness of personalized ads, marketers should invest in data-driven personalization, tailoring advertisements based on user preferences and behaviors.

Strategic Formulation: Formulate advertising strategies that leverage data insights to create personalized, relevant, and impactful ad experiences.

- b. Ad Blocker Usage and Attitudes:

Decision-Making Implications: In response to ad blocker challenges, marketers should explore alternative advertising methods and focus on creating non-intrusive, value-driven ad content.

Strategic Formulation: Formulate strategies that prioritize user experience, embracing creative formats that align with consumer preferences and mitigate ad blocker usage.

4. Content Marketing Insights:

- a. Long-Form vs. Short-Form Content:

Decision-Making Implications: Marketers should tailor content length based on target audience preferences, considering the effectiveness of both long-form and short-form content.

Strategic Formulation: Develop a content strategy that incorporates a mix of long-form and short-form content, catering to diverse audience preferences and consumption habits.

- b. Content Consumption Across Channels:

Decision-Making Implications: Understanding varied content consumption habits, marketers should optimize distribution strategies across multiple channels and devices.

Strategic Formulation: Formulate a cross-channel content distribution strategy, ensuring content is accessible and tailored to the preferences of different audience segments.

The implications derived from these research findings provide marketers with actionable insights to refine decision-making and enhance strategic formulation. By incorporating these insights into marketing strategies, professionals can navigate the evolving landscape with agility and effectively connect with their target audiences.

Chapter 20

EDUCATIONAL EMINENCE: WORLD'S TOP MARKETING SCHOOLS AND THEIR SUCCESS STORIES

Profiles of Leading Marketing Schools/Universities Globally

In the dynamic field of marketing, the role of education is pivotal in shaping the next generation of strategic thinkers and innovative marketers. This subchapter explores the profiles of leading marketing schools and universities globally, showcasing their contributions, success stories, and unique approaches to marketing education.

1. Harvard Business School (HBS):

• Overview: Renowned for its prestigious MBA program, HBS has been a trailblazer in business education. The Marketing Unit at HBS emphasizes case-based learning, immersing students in real-world marketing challenges.
• Success Stories: Graduates from HBS have gone on to lead major corporations and have played key roles in shaping marketing strategies for some of the world's most recognized brands.

2. Wharton School of the University of Pennsylvania:

• Overview: The Wharton School is a global leader in business education. Their marketing program focuses on strategic marketing management, analytics, and the integration of marketing with other business functions.
• Success Stories: Wharton alumni have excelled in various industries, contributing to the development of groundbreaking marketing strategies and holding leadership positions in top organizations.

3. London Business School (LBS):

• Overview: LBS stands as a global hub for business education. The Marketing Faculty at LBS combines rigorous academic research with practical industry insights, offering a comprehensive approach to marketing education.
• Success Stories: Graduates from LBS have made significant impacts in the marketing

landscape, influencing consumer behavior, and driving successful campaigns.

4. Kellogg School of Management, Northwestern University:

• Overview: Kellogg is renowned for its focus on marketing and its collaborative, team-oriented approach. The school emphasizes experiential learning, providing students with opportunities to work on real-world marketing projects.
• Success Stories: Kellogg alumni have achieved success in various marketing roles, contributing to the development of innovative marketing strategies and leading marketing initiatives globally.

5. INSEAD:

• Overview: With campuses in Europe, Asia, and the Middle East, INSEAD offers a global perspective on marketing education. The school's marketing curriculum emphasizes the interconnectedness of markets and the impact of cultural diversity.
• Success Stories: INSEAD alumni have become influential marketing leaders, navigating the complexities of international markets and contributing to the global marketing landscape.

6. Stanford Graduate School of Business:

• Overview: Stanford GSB is renowned for its focus on entrepreneurship and innovation. The marketing program integrates cutting-edge research with a practical understanding of how marketing drives business success.
• Success Stories: Graduates from Stanford GSB have played key roles in shaping marketing strategies for leading technology companies and have become influential figures in Silicon Valley.

7. HEC Paris:

• Overview: HEC Paris offers a unique blend of academic rigor and practical relevance in its marketing programs. The school emphasizes strategic marketing management and equips students with the skills to navigate dynamic markets.
• Success Stories: HEC Paris alumni have made significant contributions to the marketing field, leading successful marketing campaigns and driving innovation in marketing strategies.

8. ESADE Business School (Spain):

• Overview: ESADE is a prominent business school in Europe, known for its strong emphasis on innovation and entrepreneurship in marketing education. The school's marketing programs integrate academic theory with practical insights, preparing students for dynamic global markets.
• Success Stories: ESADE alumni have made notable contributions to marketing innovation and strategy, playing key roles in European and international markets.

9. Australian Graduate School of Management (AGSM):

• Overview: As a leading business school in the Asia-Pacific region, AGSM provides a comprehensive approach to marketing education, focusing on strategic marketing management and the unique challenges of the Asia-Pacific market.
• Success Stories: AGSM graduates have excelled in marketing leadership roles, influencing marketing strategies in diverse industries across the Asia-Pacific region.

10. University of Cape Town Graduate School of Business (South Africa):

• Overview. UCT GSB is a prominent business school in Africa, recognized for its commitment to responsible leadership. The marketing programs at UCT GSB emphasize understanding diverse markets and fostering sustainable marketing practices.
• Success Stories: Graduates from UCT GSB have contributed to marketing initiatives that address the unique challenges and opportunities in the African market, making a positive impact on the continent's marketing landscape.

This diverse set of leading marketing schools represents a global perspective on marketing education, showcasing institutions from Europe, Asia-Pacific, and Africa. Feel free to adjust the content to align with your book's specific focus and themes

These leading marketing schools and universities globally not only provide a strong academic foundation but also foster a culture of innovation, critical thinking, and strategic acumen. Through their success stories, these institutions continue to shape the future leaders of the marketing industry, contributing to the evolution and advancement of the field.

CLOSING REMARKS

As we conclude our journey through the foundational principles of marketing, I extend my sincerest gratitude for accompanying me on this exploration. From uncovering the intricacies of marketing strategies to unraveling the history of this dynamic discipline, we've delved into essential concepts that shape the modern business landscape.

As you close this book, remember that the knowledge you've gained serves as a compass for navigating the complexities of marketing in an ever-changing world. Whether you're a student embarking on a career in business, a seasoned professional seeking to expand your expertise, or an inquisitive mind eager to explore the nuances of marketing, I hope this journey has provided valuable insights and inspiration.

As you embark on your own marketing endeavors, remember that success lies not only in mastering the theories and techniques outlined in these pages but also in embracing creativity, adaptability, and a relentless pursuit of excellence. The field of marketing is ever-evolving, presenting new challenges and opportunities with each passing day. Embrace change, stay curious, and never cease to explore the boundless possibilities that marketing offers.

Thank you for entrusting me as your guide on this journey. May your path be illuminated by the knowledge and wisdom gained from these pages, and may your future endeavors be marked by success, innovation, and boundless creativity.

Wishing you all the best in your marketing journey!

Copyright © 2024 by Natasha Able

All rights reserved.

No part of this publication may be reproduced, distributed, or transmitted in any form or by any means, including photocopying, recording, or other electronic or mechanical methods, without the prior written permission of the publisher, except in the case of brief quotations embodied in critical reviews and certain other noncommercial uses permitted by copyright law.

www.ingramcontent.com/pod-product-compliance
Lightning Source LLC
Chambersburg PA
CBHW050117230526
45470CB00004B/1876